Puffin Books

The Puffin Book of

In 1872 the world witne

between Scotland and England in Glasgow. In 1930 Uruguay staged the first World Cup tournament, in which thirteen countries took part, and fifty-six years later, in 1986, Mexico will host the thirteenth tournament in what has become the world's most popular spectator sport.

In this history of one of the greatest sports competitions in the world, especially written for Puffin, Brian Glanville revives the memories of the early tournaments and gives an expert and detailed insight into this major event right up to the 1986 World Cup.

This is a veritable mine of information. Not only the statistics, but the atmosphere in which the games were played, outstanding players, referees, administrators, influences and incidents are excitingly recalled. The changes in the competition and the growth of tactics and techniques, from the old five-forward game to the sophisticated systems of today, are simply and clearly traced.

In the ever-changing world of sport, Brian Glanville provides a full and fascinating record of the history of international football. Anyone who reads *The Puffin Book of the World Cup* will derive a deeper interest in and understanding of the game; of how it has developed, what it has become and what may or may not happen to it in the future.

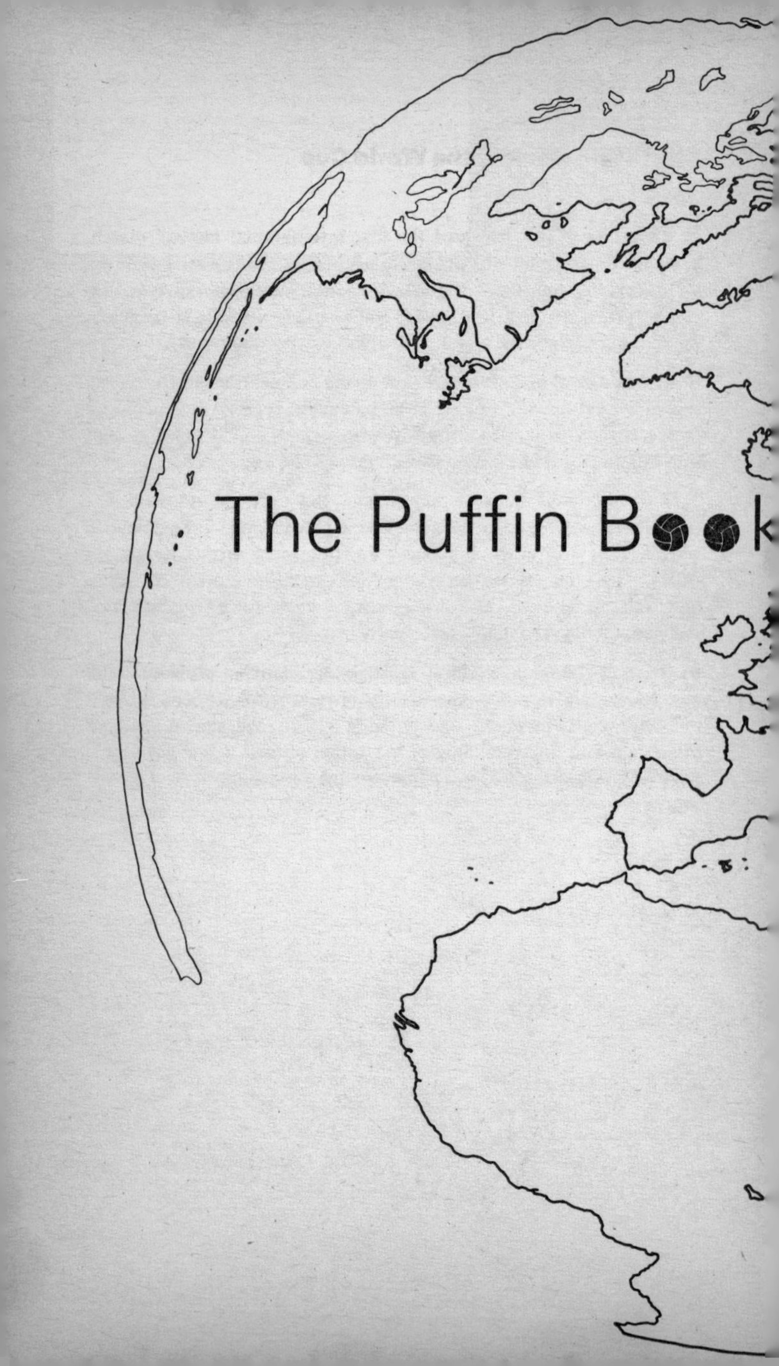
The Puffin Book

Brian Glanville

The Story of the World Cup

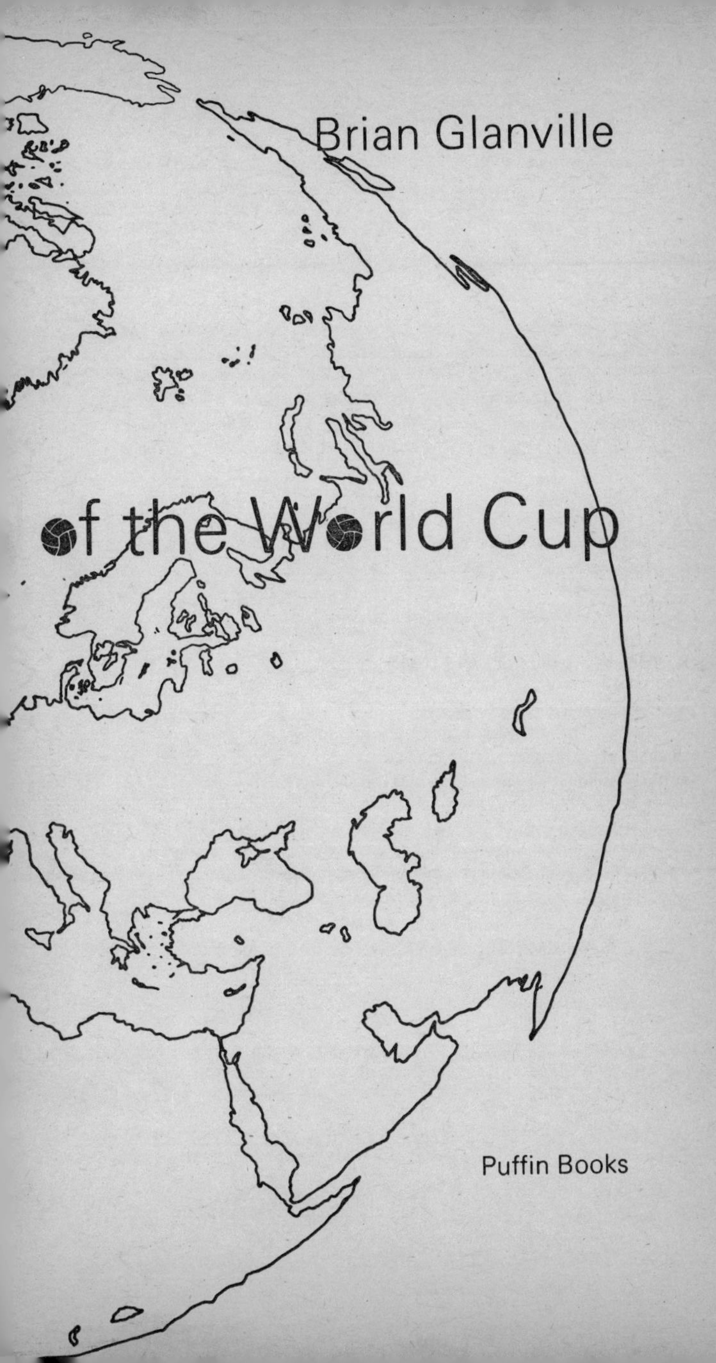

Puffin Books

Puffin Books, Penguin Books Ltd, Harmondsworth, Middlesex, England
Viking Penguin Inc., 40 West 23rd Street, New York, New York 10010, U.S.A.
Penguin Books Australia Ltd, Ringwood, Victoria, Australia
Penguin Books Canada Ltd, 2801 John Street, Markham, Ontario, Canada L3R 1B4
Penguin Books (N.Z.) Ltd, 182–190 Wairau Road, Auckland 10, New Zealand

First published 1984

All photographs used by permission of
S. & G. Press Agency Ltd, except Cruyff,
Maradona and Platini (Eamonn McCabe)

Made and printed in Great Britain by
Richard Clay (The Chaucer Press) Ltd, Bungay, Suffolk
Filmset in 9/11pt Monophoto Photina by
Northumberland Press Ltd, Gateshead, Tyne and Wear

Contents

Foreword

In 1986 Mexico will stage the thirteenth World Cup tournament. It will attract literally thousands of hours of TV air-time around the world, command the unwavering attention of millions of football fans in Europe, Asia, the Americas, Africa and probably even Antarctica. But more than this, more than the billions of pounds, dollars and pesos it will generate, the tournament will fire imaginations and inspire people everywhere, small children and their grandparents, as they witness legends being born, new names being added to the roll of honour from the past: Di Stefano, Yachine, Pelé, Cruyff, Beckenbauer and Rossi to mention but a few. The World Football Cup, rivalled only by the Olympics in its sporting appeal, will have returned, as strong and as magnetic as ever. Where did it all begin?

1 What is the World Cup?

Though it was not until 1930 that the first World Cup finals were held in Uruguay, the idea of a professional tournament was born as early as 1904 with the birth of FIFA. FIFA, founded without the benefit of British presence, is the world governing body of football, the Fédération Internationale des Football Associations, or, if you prefer, the International Federation of Association Football.

At its first meeting in Paris, FIFA decided rather grandly that they alone were entitled to organize a world championship. At that time football on the European continent was in its infancy, though British coaches were already busy teaching it abroad, but the English Football Association, true father of the game, and the other three British Associations – Scotland, Ireland and Wales – refused to have any part in FIFA. They did join briefly only to withdraw soon after the Great War, in protest over so-called 'broken time' payments to amateur players.

At FIFA's Antwerp congress in 1920, the idea of a World Cup, already much debated, was accepted in principle. In 1924 the FIFA meeting discussed it again in greater detail at the Paris Olympics, and two years later at another FIFA congress the remarkable Frenchman, Henri Delaunay, who was Secretary of the French Football Federation from 1919 till his death in 1956, announced, 'Today, international football can no longer be held within the confines of the Olympics; and many countries where professionalism is now recognized and organized cannot any longer be represented there by their best players.'

That hit the nail on the head and brought the World Cup a good deal nearer. Ever since 1908, when the first four-yearly Olympic Games were held at the specially built White City Stadium in West London, there had been an Olympic football tournament.

Inevitably, the powerful United Kingdom team, made up chiefly of genuine amateurs who played regularly in the League for professional clubs (quite a common thing in those days), dominated the competition. But both in 1908 in London and in 1912 in Stockholm, they were given a tremendous run for their money in the Final by the full Danish international team. The Danes too were all amateurs: big, strong fellows, who had taken to the new game with astonishing enthusiasm and success. Indeed after the war one of their players, the towering half-back Nils Middelboe, went on to captain Chelsea in the English First Division.

By the time the Olympic Games started again in Antwerp in 1920, continental football had made amazing strides. The four British countries, as we have seen, were no longer competing and it is doubtful whether by then even a team made up of the best players from all four countries could have won the tournament. The game had spread with phenomenal speed in both Europe and South America and although professionalism was not recognized officially, it was no secret that many, perhaps even most, of the leading players were paid footballers.

By 1924, when a superb Uruguayan team came to Paris and took the tournament, professionalism was less the exception than the rule. Tiny little Uruguay somehow managed to produce teams which were the equal and envy of their far bigger neighbours such as Brazil. Playing splendid, fast, highly skilled, exciting football, with wonderful forwards such as Petrone and Scarone – a pale, slender, red-haired figure – an attacking centre-half in Gestido and an excellent half-back in the black Andrade (whose nephew would be a great World Cup star of the fifties), Uruguay kept the Cup in 1928. But this time it took a replay with the similarly talented Argentines for them to do so.

Fulvio Bernardini, a university graduate from Rome, who played attacking centre-half for Italy and later became a famous club manager, played in the 1924 tournament and subsequently wrote that it was unfair that other countries should be blamed for using professionals: 'After all,' he asked, 'what were *we*?'

It was perfectly plain that the game had simply grown too big for the Olympic tournament and that some alternative professional competition was required to absorb it. Some countries, like Britain, took an honest, straightforward line and would not enter their full, professional, international teams in what was strictly an amateur tournament. Others felt able to use some but not all of their players as amateurs.

As so often in the history of international football, the drive, inspiration and determination which created the World Cup came from France. It was the idea of two men, pioneers of French football: the industrious Delaunay (mentioned above) and the equally dedicated and far-seeing Jules Rimet, President of the French Federation, after whom the cup was eventually named. Indeed, until the Brazilians won it for the third time in Mexico in 1970, it was incorrect to call it anything but the Jules Rimet Trophy, though everybody knew it was in fact the World Cup.

In 1928, after Britain had withdrawn from FIFA and Uruguay had won their second title in Amsterdam, Delaunay put up a motion for a world tournament. It was passed; all that had still to be decided was where it should be played.

In the event, Uruguay's claims to play host outweighed those of Italy, Holland, Spain and Sweden, all of whom, with the exception of Holland, have since hosted a World Cup. 'Other countries have their history,' said Ondino Viera, the wise and dedicated Uruguayan team manager, at the 1966 World Cup in Britain, 'Uruguay has its football.'

For a little country – though rich in beef – Uruguay made a remarkable offer to the footballing world. In a mere eight months they would build a wholly new stadium in Montevideo for the competition. They did and called it the Centenary Stadium in celebration of a hundred years of independence from the Spanish colonists. They also offered to pay all the fares and travelling expenses for the visiting teams.

Thereafter, the World Cup was held every four years like the Olympic Games, with which it can be compared in more ways than one. For just as no truly great athlete, even one like Roger Bannister, who first ran the four minute mile, can claim to have touched the peaks unless he's won an Olympic gold medal, so the World Cup has become what Delaunay and Rimet wanted it to be – the true touchstone, the ultimate goal of international football. A team which has won the World Cup will be remembered as long as the game is played. A player who has shone in the World Cup can claim to be great; though some players, like George Best of Northern Ireland, though great in their day, were prevented from ever playing in a World Cup by the comparative weakness of their national team at the time.

The word 'Cup' properly suggests a knock-out competition. The first major competition in the history of football, the F.A. Cup, was designed on those lines after the model of the so-called Cock House Cup at Harrow School and 'sudden death' was its essence. Two teams met. The winner went on to the next round, the loser fell out of the tournament and so it continued until there was only one team left, winner of the trophy.

With the exception of 1934 in Italy and 1938 in France, the World Cup has never been played on that basis. Indeed, it has sometimes been difficult to be sure on exactly what basis it has been played. You can sympathize with the World Cup's organizers, in their continual attempts to reconcile the idea of Cup football with some notion of justice and logic. For the heart of Cup football, its true attraction, is surely its very lack of logic, its element of surprise, of David against Goliath. Yet when you get an extraordinary result, such as the United States of America beating England in Belo Horizonte, Brazil, in 1950, North Korea beating Italy at Middlesbrough in 1966, or Algeria beating West Germany in Gijón, Spain, in 1982, it still seems vaguely wrong when such winners then fall by the wayside; the Americans and Algerians in the very first stage, the North Koreans admittedly not until the quarter-finals, while the West Germans, despite having lost to the Algerians, were able to go on to the Final of the 1982 competition.

More contradictory still – in 1954 West Germany beat Hungary in the Final in Berne, Switzerland, after having lost to them by a shattering 8–3 in the first round of the competition! And again in 1974 they lost in Hamburg, on their own territory, to East Germany, yet went on to win the Final against Holland in Munich. Ideally it should not be possible for a beaten team ever to win a Cup competition, but in the World Cup, as you see, it can happen.

In 1930, a World Cup involving only thirteen countries (as, astoundingly enough, it would again twenty years later) was at first divided into four pools of little leagues, the four winners of which went straight into the semi-finals. This was the first World Cup compromise, a tournament which went knock-out in its second, semi-final stage, but retained a league pattern, with its supposedly greater fairness and 'logic', in the opening phase.

As we have seen, the 1934 and 1938 World Cups were knock-out tournaments on a straightforward, sudden-death pattern. They weren't in any way 'fair' and they threw up plenty of pleasing surprises. The trouble was that they also meant that teams such as Argentina and Brazil, in the 1934 tournament, could sail thousands of miles across the Atlantic from the New World to the Old, play one match, lose, then sail immediately thousands of miles back again.

It was the immense problem of time and distance which made the first World Cup such a second-rate and poorly attended one. None of the four countries which had contested the honour of putting on the first World Cup with Uruguay made the long journey, nor did Austria or Hungary, two of the best teams in Europe at the time, each country having been splendidly coached by a little Lancashireman called Jimmy Hogan, who had gone out to teach them before the Great War, and who had learned his principles of the game from Scottish players as a young professional at Fulham.

The Uruguayans had been terribly put out when their beloved tournament was snubbed by so many teams. The British, still not members of FIFA, had not been eligible anyway. But Uruguay took offence and refused to compete in either of the two European tournaments before the Second World War, though some said their decision was also affected by the fact that their best players had a tendency to go on strike. As for the Argentines, they deliberately sent a weakened team to Italy in 1934, furious that the Italians had 'stolen' two of their best players of the 1930 World Cup: Luisito Monti, the tough, attacking centre-half, and Raimondo Orsi, the fast left-winger. Both had played for Argentina against Uruguay in the 1930 World Cup Final and were there again in the 1934 Final, but playing for Italy. Both were of Italian descent and could therefore claim double nationality.

In 1950, by which time the tournament had gone back to South

America – it's now played alternately in Europe and America – a new formula was devised. A strange one.

People talk about Uruguay winning the 1950 World Cup Final against Brazil in front of 200,000 people at the Maracana Stadium, in Rio. In fact, though it was the decisive match and a wonderful one, worthy of any World Cup Final, it was not actually the Final. There wasn't one!

The thirteen teams (again!) were divided, very unevenly indeed, into four qualifying pools, as they had been in 1930. This time, however, there were no semi-finals. Instead, stubbornly applying league principles to what was supposed to be a cup competition, it was decided that the four teams which won their groups would not play knock-out semi-finals as they had in 1930. Instead they would go into yet another group, the Final Pool. This too was played on the customary league basis of two points for a win, one for a draw, with so-called goal average (goals scored divided by goals against) as the decider should two teams finish level on points.

By a happy freak of chance the last day of the competition left Brazil, the hosts and red-hot favourites, with four points from two games – won by smashing scores of 6–1 and 7–1 against Spain and Sweden – playing Uruguay, who had three points and a hopelessly inferior goal average. Thus all Brazil had to achieve was a draw, which, on the form shown up to that point, looked a pretty easy task. Indeed to most neutral observers, anything but a Brazilian win seemed out of the question and the prospect that Uruguay might actually turn form on its head by winning seemed utterly remote.

But win they did in a shock worthy of any cup tie. Indeed, although they went behind early in the second half, Brazil never really had the upper hand and Uruguay were able to cap a glorious defensive action with two wonderful breakaway goals by the slender inside-left, Juan Schiaffino, and the hunched little right-winger, Alcide 'Chico' Ghiggia. Of such surprises are great World Cup memories made, but you could hardly thank those who devised the competition for that. It occurred in spite of them.

In 1954, when a most exciting and dazzling World Cup was played in Switzerland, the organizers came up with an even sillier scheme. True, the old idea of the knock-out competition was more closely followed than it had been since 1938; there would be sudden-death quarter-finals as well as semi-finals, culminating in a proper Final. But to get to those quarter-finals, what a weird madman's flytrap of a system had to be negotiated!

At least on this occasion all sixteen teams had the goodness to turn up. In 1950, Scotland, in an incredible fit of pique, had refused to go to Brazil even though they had qualified by coming second in the British Championship, a competition which was most generously used as a qualifying group for *two* teams. They wouldn't deign to cross the Atlantic, they said, unless they actually won the British title. As it was they lost 1–0 to England in the final and decisive game in Glasgow, after actually hitting the English crossbar. It was as close as that. Billy Wright, the stocky, blond Wolves wing-half who captained England in three World Cups, begged George Young, the Scottish captain, to do his best to persuade the Scottish officials to let them go; he thought it would be a great help to England. Young tried, but he failed.

The Czechs, too, refused to go to Brazil. The French at first agreed to go, but when they saw the programme they would have to follow and the colossal distances they would have to cover, they changed their minds and stayed at home. How strange it all seems now, when countries fall over themselves to get into the World Cup finals. Indeed the main reason the European nations agreed to a bloated twenty-four team World Cup from 1982 onwards was because it would give them a double chance of qualifying in their eliminating groups.

As it was, in Brazil, Uruguay were left with only one eliminating match to play and that against the feeble Bolivians whom they beat 8–0, thus arriving fresh and spruce in the Final Pool. Other teams by contrast were obliged to traipse all over the massive country to play their qualifying games; with the exception of Brazil, who merely had to play one match out of Rio, in the not too remote São Paolo.

Nowadays, at least, qualifying groups play within the same, relatively small, area.

The Swiss World Cup then did at least feature four initial qualifying groups of four, but what an odd and perverse pattern each group was obliged to follow! Instead of each team playing the other three, each team played only two others, making it only too likely that two teams would finish level on points. Since it would have been ridiculous to decide on goal average after a mere two matches, it was laid down that teams which finished level on points would have to play off. This meant that these unfortunate teams had to play an extra game to see who would qualify for the quarter-finals; it could also mean them having to play a team they had played once already, with all the bad feeling that may have built up.

Such was the case when in Pool IV, Switzerland, the hosts, who had already beaten Italy 2–1, had to play them again, after losing to England, who had won the group. The first game had been hot-tempered enough, even though it was played in the delightful lakeside setting of Lausanne. What a game it was when the Italians and Swiss clashed – and that was the word for it – a second time.

The Swiss, less skilled than the Italians, made up for that with their energy and determination. It was a game which needed a good referee but, alas, like so many games in the history of the World Cup, it did not get one. The Brazilian referee, Viana, had little control. 'An English or Scottish referee,' wrote Gabriel Hanot, a famous French journalist, manager and player, the inventor of the European Cup for clubs, 'would have given two or three penalties in the first half against the Swiss and would have sent off the two Italian backs, Vincenzi and Giacomazzi, in the second.'

Italy grew tired of the way their clever forwards, Carlo Galli and Giampiero Boniperti, later the President of the famous Juventus club, were being knocked down or obstructed. In the end they took the law into their own hands with drastic results. One Swiss player, the little left-winger Jacky Fatton, was kicked in the stomach, another in the back.

Halfway through the second half, another Italian forward, Benito Lorenzi, nicknamed 'Poison' for his quick temper, scored what seemed a perfectly fair goal, which would have put Italy in the lead. Viana disallowed it for offside, but since Lorenzi scored after Galli had driven Pandolfini's pass against a post, this seemed a very odd decision. Some thought it was simply Viana's way of showing he had had enough of Lorenzi's endless protests.

As the leading Italian newspaper, the *Corriere della Sera*, put it, one then 'witnessed one of those scenes which often occur on our grounds, the players swarming round the referee, some tearing their hair, some eating the grass in their desperation'. But Viana would not relent, the goal was disallowed and thus when Giacomazzi made a defensive blunder the Swiss were able, through Hugi, to score the winner.

Who would have wanted to referee the play-off? The Italians had played awfully well to beat the Belgians 4–1, but back on their home ground, it was the familiar tale of squabbles and lack of discipline. It would take the calming influence of Enzo Bearzot, the lean, dark, pipe-smoking manager from Friule, in the North East, to calm the team in training camp in 1978 and 1982, and finally, in Spain, to take it to its first title since 1938. 'Uncle' Lajos Czeizler, the elderly Hungarian who had somewhat unexpectedly been put in command of the explosive 1954 team, had no such control. There were, it was sombrely reported, 'open acts of indiscipline'.

Czeizler picked a very odd team for the play-off and very oddly it played, going 2–0 down to a Swiss team which dominated the game. The Italians did not do so badly in the first half and were only one goal behind at half-time. But a couple of minutes into the second half, the lively Ballaman headed in a corner and Italy cracked, and though they did get one goal back some twenty minutes later, they gave away two more in the final five minutes to lose by an embarrassing 4–1.

In Pool II, however, there was a still stranger story. Germany, who were playing their first World Cup since 1938 – they had been refused permission to compete in 1950 as a mark of disapproval of their role in the Second World War – easily beat Turkey in their opening game, while Hungary, the brilliant favourites, scored nine goals against a feeble South Korea.

With superb attacking inside-forwards in Sandor Kocsis, known as 'Golden Head' for his power in the air, Ferenc Puskas, an inside-left with a wonderful left foot, and a skilled, deep-lying centre-forward in Nandor Hidegkuti, plus a driving, attacking right-half in Jozef Bozsik, Hungary had been easily the best team in Europe for several years.

In 1952, fielding their full international side, they had warmed up by winning the Olympic tournament in Helsinki. In November 1953, they had gone to Wembley and, with a 6–3 victory, had smashed England's record of having never been beaten at home by a foreign team. Hidegkuti not only scored a magnificent goal in ninety seconds, but was to score twice more before the end of the match. The following May, Hungary rubbed salt in the wound by thrashing England 7–1 in Budapest.

Now Sepp Herberger, the tough little manager who had taken over the German team on the eve of the 1938 World Cup, following their crushing 6–3 defeat by England in Berlin, reasoned that there was no need for his team to waste its energy against Hungary; at least the first time around. Defeat, by even the highest of scores, would make no odds. The play-off would be against Turkey again, and would be simply a formality.

So the Germans put out a team which included several reserves, and when their big, blond centre-half, Werner Liebrich, kicked the Hungarian Puskas, possibly by accident, it could have been said to be the kick that eventually won the 1954 World Cup. Puskas couldn't play again until the Final, and even then he was manifestly not fit. The Germans lost to Hungary 8–3 in Basel, Kocsis getting four of the goals; whereupon they made seven changes – and scored seven goals against Turkey in the play-off. The strange and unpredictable system of the competition, however, brought Germany and Hungary together again in the Final, where Germany scored another three goals, and Hungary only two, giving Germany the title – a little unfairly one might think.

The next four World Cups were more reasonably organized. Four qualifying pools – in Sweden, Chile, England and Mexico – produced eight quarter-finalists (the first and second in each group qualifying), who were divided into two pools, and each team now played all three teams in their pool. In Sweden, by a curious chance, all three British teams involved had to play off, since all three had shared second place, finishing level on both points and goals with an opponent. Of the three, Wales (who had come in at the last moment, beating Israel in an extra eliminator, after all Israel's adversaries had withdrawn on political grounds) knocked out Hungary, gallant Northern Ireland, splendid conquerors of Italy in the qualifiers, defeated the Czechs, but England went down to Russia.

England's team had been badly weakened after three of their finest players, Roger Byrne, the captain and left-back, Duncan Edwards, a massive, dominant, twenty-one-year-old left-half and Tommy Taylor, a most effective centre-forward, died in the snow at Munich Airport, when Manchester United's Elizabethan aircraft crashed on the way back from a European Cup match in Belgrade. And when the brilliant left-winger Tom Finney, with his beautiful swerve and inimitable footwork, was hurt in the opening game against Russia, the side's chances became slimmer still.

The game against Russia, a most exciting one held in Gothenburg, was drawn 2–2, after the big centre-forward Derek Kevan outjumped the even bigger Russian goalkeeper, Lev Yachine, for a thrilling equalizer. But in the replay England most surprisingly threw in two young players, inside-right Peter Broadbent and outside-right Peter Brabrook, for their very first international caps and Russia won with a shot by Ivanov which went in off the post.

Broadbent and Brabrook cannot be held entirely to blame however for England's defeat. Few of the team were on top form and the fact that Fulham and Blackburn Rovers had just been engaged in a fierce and exhausting struggle to emerge from the Second Division had clearly left its mark on Johnny Haynes, the young Londoner whose superb cross-field and through passing made him the key man in attack; on Bobby Robson, his inside-forward partner at Fulham; and on Blackburn's talented little right-winger, Bryan Douglas; while Ronnie Clayton, Blackburn's captain and right-half, had only gained a place in the group's play-off.

Northern Ireland, too, had suffered from the Munich air crash, notably in the loss of Jackie Blanchflower, their elegant, mobile, adventurous centre-half, who first played as an inside-forward. He was not killed, fortunately, but was so badly affected by the appalling disaster that he would never play again.

This had a severe effect on the fine Irish team which had superbly beaten Italy in Belfast, after their first World Cup match against Italy, early in the year, had been played as a hot-blooded friendly, because the Hungarian referee, Istvan Zsolt, was held up by fog. At the end of the game the crowd invaded the pitch, but Danny Blanchflower, Jackie's older brother, the gifted captain of the team, fluent as both speaker and footballer, told every member of his side to escort an Italian player to safety,

Harry Gregg, the big, brave, Irish goalkeeper, had been the true hero of the Munich crash, risking his life by dragging people out of the wreckage. He would play a marvellous game against Germany in a 2–2 draw in the World Cup.

In the event, an exhausted and depleted Irish team would lose in the quarter finals 4–0 to the French, while Wales would lose, most unluckily, after a gallant display in Gothenburg, to Brazil, and a freakish goal by the seventeen-year-old Pelé. The shot hit the boot of the Welsh full-back, Stuart Williams, and was deflected past their excellent goalkeeper, Arsenal's Jack Kelsey.

In the 1974 competition changes were made again, for no obvious good reason. They were ill-judged changes which did not, however, reveal the full extent of their folly until the 1978 tournament in Argentina. Then it became clear that unless teams were splendidly and excitingly prepared to attack, as were the 'Total Football' playing teams of 1974 with their all-purpose players, boredom could set in; negative play would be the order of the day. The situation was perhaps best described by the clever, dark Italian outside-right, Franco Causio, after a dreary draw with West Germany in Buenos Aires: 'The West Germans built the Berlin Wall in Argentina.'

The new pattern of the competition was clearly another misguided attempt to somehow turn a World Cup into a kind of miniature league tournament. Once again there would be four initial qualifying groups, producing as usual eight survivors. But these would no longer go into the quarter-finals. There wouldn't be any. Instead, there would be two further groups of four teams, with the winning teams of each group going on to contest the Final. Once again, great ingenuity had been used to produce a fatuous result.

As the tournament went on and tension grew – at least, in Argentina – the incentive to win produced by a knock-out tournament was replaced by the careful calculation typical of league play.

But far worse was the scandal of the game between Argentina and Peru in the final match of the second round in Rosario. After a wretched beginning in the seaside resort of Mar del Plata, where, on an appalling, divot-ridden pitch, they were very lucky to qualify, Brazil had improved greatly. They played a harsh and bruising draw with Argentina in which some frightening fouls took place and no goals were scored, they had no trouble beating Peru and, in their last game, they faced Poland. At that stage Brazil and Argentina were level on points, neck and neck. But by an inept piece of planning, Brazil's game was scheduled to take place in the afternoon, Argentina's not until the evening.

This meant that by the time Argentina played Peru, they would know the result of the Brazil–Poland match, and would consequently know not only what result they would need to reach the Final, but even how many goals they would have to win by *if* they had to win.

In the event Brazil, with their little inside-left Dirceu in splendid form, thrashed Poland 3–1, which set the Argentines a hard task. They had to beat Peru by at least four goals to qualify. Indeed, the odds seemed to favour Brazil. The Peruvians began pretty well, having the best of the early play and even hitting the post. Then, almost mysteriously, they fell apart. They seemed to lose strength and heart, and were annihilated 6–0, sending Argentina through to the Final, in which they would eventually and excitingly beat Holland. But the Brazilians were furious. They made it plain they believed the match was a 'fix', that the Peruvians had been paid to lose by so many goals, and indeed rumours were rife. 'In the next World Cup,' said Claudio Coutinho, the doomed and handsome manager of Brazil, who, alas, drowned before that tournament, 'the Peruvians will not be able to hear their national anthem played with pride.'

That match still gives off a very fishy odour, and it must be admitted that the way the last two games were staggered lent itself almost as if by design to suspicions and possibilities of this kind. There is an old saying that justice must not only be done, it must be seen to be done. It had certainly not been seen to be done in 1978.

Then came the first 'monster' World Cup, a World Cup with not sixteen but twenty-four teams; an awkward number in every way.

The idea of sixteen teams came from the old notion of a knock-out competition in which teams took part in multiples of four: sixteen, thirty-two, even sixty-four. With twenty-four teams, the competition not only became much longer and greatly diluted in quality, it also became unwieldy. What did you do with the twenty-four teams?

The solution used in Spain in 1982, which proved to be a poor one, was first to divide the twenty-four teams into six groups with four teams in each group. The teams in the first two places in each group would then advance to the so-called second round, which would be made up of four groups of three teams each, again played on a league basis, and the four winners would at last go into the semi-finals, played as knock-out games. But the competition was so long and so drawn-out, not only by the size of the entry but because the games were often played, in the same group, on consecutive days instead of the same day, that in the end there was neither room nor time to replay any semi-final which might be drawn, as one indeed was.

But to go back to the first round ... This produced one perfectly disgraceful game, though to be quite fair it might have taken place in all but the 1934 and 1938 'sudden-death' tournaments, had teams been as cynical and unsporting as West Germany and Austria were on this occasion.

In their group, the West Germans, amazingly, had been beaten 2–1 in Gijón by the utterly unfancied Algerians. Austria, however, beat the Algerians and by the time they were due to play West Germany in the final game of the group, they had four points, from two wins, to West Germany's two.

Early in the match, which was also played in Gijón, little Pierre Littbarski, the clever German winger, crossed a ball from the left which the centre-forward, Horst Hrubesch, headed into the Austrian goal. From that moment on the game degenerated into the kind of match a boxing referee would have stopped and declared no contest, disqualifying both competitors for lack of effort. It was quite clear that some kind of non-aggression pact had been made. Michel Hidalgo, the French team manager, who had come along to watch because his team was likely to play one or the other of the two sides, said afterwards that he had not taken a single note, adding wryly that the game should be awarded the Nobel Peace Prize.

The Algerians were rightly furious, but the World Cup Committee took no notice of their protests, and Herr Neuberger, its West German representative, who was usually the first to roar his disapproval and lay down the law, was surprisingly mild when questioned in the Gijón stadium after the match. Later FIFA would talk about enacting rules to punish such displeasing play in the future; but that did not help the unlucky Algerians.

So the West Germans went on into a group which included England and Spain, in Madrid. In the opening match with England they played an appallingly dull and dreary draw. Once again, the fact that league rather than cup principles were at work meant that teams could go out to play for a draw, rather than a victory. The West Germans stiffened their defence and scarcely bothered to try to win.

As for England, they gave themselves away the following morning when, in the sunlit Press Conference at Navacerada, outside Madrid, Ron Greenwood, the England team manager, cheerfully accused the journalists of not having given England credit for one of their greatest achievements. What was that, he was asked? Why, he said, they'd prevented Manny Kaltz from getting in any crosses.

Nobody could believe their ears. Manny Kaltz, for goodness' sake, was the German right-back; and there were England using their left-back, Kenny Sansom, and their deep-lying left-winger, Graham Rix, chiefly to stifle him, a defender! When Italy played and beat West Germany in the Final, they hardly bothered about Kaltz at all. They simply kept him busy chasing their own attackers.

Then came the ill-fated semi-final in Seville between West Germany and France. In the first place, it was daft to play it in Seville instead of Madrid, where both teams had qualified. After all, Italy and Poland were able to play their semi-final in the massive Nou Camp Stadium in Barcelona, the city where they had both qualified. On top of that, the game was played in the evening, thus giving the players less recovery time than those who played in the Barcelona semi-final, which took place in the afternoon – a point which should not be under-rated, particularly as the Seville game went into extra time. The French built up a 3–1 lead in the first extra-time period, but a brutal foul by Harald Schumacher, the German keeper, on their defender, Battiston, early in the second half of normal time, had disrupted them and as Battiston himself had only just come on as a tactical substitution, in replacing him they had to use up their second and last substitute far too early. Add to that a highly doubtful goal by Rummenigge, the clever but injured German forward, who came on early in extra time, and you will see that the French had cause to feel displeased.

Ultimately, West Germany forced a 3–3 draw. And as there was no time for a replay, the teams were obliged to decide the semi-final – the World Cup semi-final! – on penalty kicks which, 'like the flowers that bloom in the Spring, tra-la', as the song goes, had no bearing on the previous 120 minutes' play.

There is clearly something very wrong with the organization of a tournament which takes two years, including its qualifying competition, to complete, yet which allows no time for a replay at the very late, enormously important, semi-final stage. In effect, the West Germany–France semi-final was decided on chance. How else can you describe a result based on penalty kicks? You might just as well have tossed a coin, as, unbelievably, had been the plan in 1970, if the Final had resulted in a draw after a replay.

So the Germans, missing only one penalty while the French missed two, went into the World Cup Final; but the occasion left a very sour taste.

After this highly unsatisfactory conclusion to the semi-final, the unhappy players then had to put up with utter chaos at the airport of Seville; further proof of the sheer idiocy of moving the match from Madrid. Hundreds of people struggled and scrambled in the small hours of the morning to get on a flight back to the Spanish capital.

Paul Breitner, the West German captain and inside-forward, already a star full-back in the 1974 World Cup, was enraged. In perfect Spanish – he had played for Real Madrid – he violently criticized what he called the wretched disorganization of the tournament. The Spanish newspapers called his outburst 'scandalous', but to everybody else, the scandal plainly lay in the hopeless arrangements.

Michel Hidalgo, the modest, pleasant, French team manager, was later as critical as Breitner, if somewhat less fiery. It was monstrous, he complained, that 'players were obliged to sit on their suitcases, while plane after plane took off'.

So the West Germans arrived back in Madrid at an unearthly hour, tired out not only by the 120 minutes of the semi-final, with its enormous physical and nervous strain, but also by the ridiculous aftermath at Seville Airport.

Yet it wasn't the first time there had been confusion and controversy over air travel at a World Cup semi-final, though the previous occasion had had its lighter side.

That was in the French World Cup in 1938, when air travel was a much less common, much less available, means of travel than in the jet age of today. Italy, under the multi-lingual, commanding Vittorio Pozzo, had been drawn against Brazil, in Marseilles. The Final was due to be played shortly afterwards in Paris.

When Pozzo and his team arrived in Marseilles, they discovered that the Brazilians, in their supreme confidence, had fully booked the only aeroplane available to take people back to Paris.

Pozzo went to see them, pointing out that the semi-final had not yet been played, the Brazilians had not yet reached the Final. But we shall, they told him, with innocent assurance. '*Già scontato?* Already decided?' asked Pozzo. 'Already decided,' answered the Brazilians, who then, in their strange arrogance, decided to leave out their two finest forwards, Leonidas, the so-called Black Diamond, and Tim, who, as an old man, would manage the Peruvian team which reached the 1982 World Cup finals.

As it turned out, the Italians won the game, leaving the Brazilians to play in the Third Place match in Bordeaux; but there was still no room on the plane and little on the train. The Italian players had to stand, almost all the way to Paris.

2 The Centre-Forwards

Some people will tell you that nothing ever really changes in football, but one thing that has changed over the past twenty years is its terminology. A goalkeeper, of course, is always a goalkeeper; what else could he ever be? A full-back is still a full-back, even if he now has a more adventurous and attacking role – very much like the old style wing-half, in the days before the offside law changed in 1925 and the stopper centre-half was born.

Centre-half? We have to learn nowadays to call them centre-backs, and there tend to be two of them where once there was only one. Wing-halves and inside-forwards, as they used to be called before the Brazilians invented the 4-2-4 plan and brought it to the 1958 World Cup in Sweden, are now generally classified just as midfield players: though the Brazilians themselves have always drawn a distinction between the two roles.

Up front, we are meant to believe that we can no longer talk about wingers, attacking inside-forwards and centre-forwards, only about something called a striker (an animal as mythical to me as the unicorn), supposed to be able to do anything in attack which was once done either on the flanks, down the middle, or alongside the centre-forward, by the relevant specialist player.

Then along comes somebody like Horst Hrubesch, the massive West German, star of the 1980 European Championship in Italy, goalscorer in the 1982 World Cup in Spain, and proof that of course the centre-forward still exists – Hrubesch could be nothing else; just as little Pierre Littbarski, who created Hrubesch's goal against Austria in Gijón in 1982, could be nothing but a winger.

Not only was Hrubesch plainly a centre-forward, he was also plainly the old-fashioned type of centre-forward, or 'target man', basing his game on an exceptionally powerful physique, his height and his ability to climb above the defence and score goals in the air. That kind of player was well known in Britain, especially in the days of the 'W' formation, with its system of placing two wingers and a centre-forward upfield, and two inside-forwards to supply them behind. He was not unknown even before the Great War.

But as football grew 'modern', more mobile and supposedly more scientific, the 'target man' became something of an object of ridicule. He seemed out of date, a bit of a dinosaur, a blunt instrument and, in some opinions, an easy option. Players who lacked creative skill and imagination, as the British were often said to do, had only to bang the ball down the middle or across the goal at their Goliath of a centre-forward and leave him to get on with it. Yet the success of Hrubesch, who was twenty-nine years old before he made a name with Hamburg and played for West Germany, showed that this kind of player could be enormously effective, even in the team which in 1970 had pioneered 'Total Football' and produced the astonishing, quite different, but deadly effective Gerd Muller at centre-forward.

Centre-forwards, then, still quite definitely exist, even if they are not all like Hrubesch, as indeed they have never been. They come in all shapes and sizes. They can be as big as Hrubesch, as small as Paolo Rossi with his six marvellous goals and superb contribution to winning the 1982 World Cup. They can be as lean, mobile and wiry as Johan Cruyff, the magnificent Dutch captain who played in the Final of the 1974 World Cup and secured a first-minute penalty, and who would surely have won the 1978 tournament for Holland had he only agreed to take part. They can be as elegant, elusive and deadly as Ademir, leading goalscorer of the 1950 World Cup and perhaps the finest centre-forward Brazil has ever had. They can be as unorthodox as little Raymond Kopa, another beautifully balanced player, once an outside-right, operating cleverly behind his front runners in Sweden in 1958 and making goal after goal with his clever dribbling and superb, defence-splitting passing. Or they can be like Silvio Piola, almost as great an Italian hero in the 1938 World Cup for Italy as Paolo Rossi was in 1982, a very big man with the skills and agility of a smaller man, a player who could be physically tough or wonderfully delicate, whose most famous goal of all was probably the one he punched against

England in Milan in 1939 and which Dr Pecos Bauwens, the German referee, allowed to stand.

The story of Rossi and his uneven, finally dazzling, performance in the 1982 World Cup is one of the most remarkable stories of the competition. It was Rossi's second World Cup and he had done exceptionally well in his first, four years earlier, in Argentina. Born in the Tuscan city of Prato, he had not had an easy start. He played at first for a little local team called Cattolica Virtus, a 'nursery' team of the mighty, wealthy Turin club, Juventus, as did his brother, who was actually a centre-forward, while Rossi began as an outside-right.

As such he went to Juventus and Turin, was put in the first team squad, but never got a game. Juventus put him out on loan to Como, a club with a lovely lakeside setting, but with little chance of staying in the First Division.

Rossi, always a boyish, cheerful, good-natured figure, played a few league games without success, had serious trouble with his cartilage, which required surgery, and was put out on loan again; this time to Lanerossi Vicenza, in the Second Division.

Things now began to happen. It was there that a manager called Fabbri cured him of what he called his 'dribbling mania', and turned him into a centre-forward. With amazing success. Rossi scored twenty-one goals and Lanerossi were promoted. Juventus obviously didn't take Serie B, the Second Division, very seriously. They could have had Rossi back, but instead they left him in Vicenza for another year. Whereupon the now twenty-two-year-old Rossi, playing for a minor team against the giants in a deeply defensive championship, rattled off another twenty-four goals.

Now Juventus wanted him back; but Vicenza had a half share to buy out and Vicenza wanted him too. There was an 'auction', bids were made in sealed envelopes and, to the general stupor, Vicenza far outbid the rich and powerful Juventus. They offered a colossal £1.5 million for their half of Rossi, who thus, barely fledged as an international player, went to Argentina, valued at three million pounds. It would, in time, be his undoing.

For the moment, however, all was splendour. Rossi was picked for the World Cup team at once. Lively, wonderfully quick in thought and movement, he danced past defenders and combined beautifully with his fellow forwards, especially the skilful, silver-haired Roberto Bettega. Above all, he had an amazing nose for a chance. Somehow he seemed able to drift, time and again, into the right position, into open space, unnoticed and unmarked, getting to the ball first not only with his foot but, more surprisingly, with his head.

Goals, such as those he so dramatically scored in Spain against Brazil, Poland in the semi-final and West Germany in the Final, were not the classic centre-forward's headed goals, scored with mighty jumps above a straining defence. They were the result of sudden, rapid runs into the penalty box, to meet centres both at the near and far posts, goals flicked in while defenders were still wondering where on earth this player had come from.

In 1978, he got a goal on the frightful pitch at Mar del Plata in the opening game against France. A kind of pin-table goal, the ball ricocheting about in the penalty area. In the third game, to be played against Argentina in the huge River Plate Stadium with its passionate crowd, Rossi was going to be rested. Instead, he insisted on playing, saying he was perfectly fit and if there were any reason for leaving him out he would like to know it. So he played and worked out a wonderful, winning goal with Bettega, perhaps the most skilfully fashioned goal of the whole tournament. Racing out to the left he began the movement with a typical burst of speed, brought off a dazzling exchange of first-time passes with Bettega and sent Bettega through to slip the ball past Ubaldo Fillol into the net.

On the same ground, Rossi also scored a splendid, winning goal against Austria. Saucily crossing his legs, Rossi sent Franco Causio away down the left wing then, with another of his typical bursts of pace, he left the heavy, blond Austrian sweeper, Obermayer, toiling in the rear and beat Koncilia in the Austrian goal. Defeat by Holland, however, put Italy out of the competition, though in that game, too, Rossi contributed to the Italian goal, his pressing presence causing Erny Brandts, the Dutch centre-back, to slide in and beat his own goalkeeper.

Rossi went home a hero, subjected to all the hysterical ardour Italian fans reserve for their footballing idols. At Rome Airport, he was so besieged by Press and television alike he wasn't even able to see his own parents. In the following season, however, things began to go wrong. Vicenza slipped badly, Rossi lost form, the team were relegated and Lanerossi had to sell him.

The trouble was that nobody would buy him; he was simply too expensive even for the richest clubs. Only Naples bid and Rossi, knowing the wild fervour of that pulsating city, would not go there. The best Lanerossi could do was put him out on loan to Perugia, another unfashionable, provincial club that was having a moment of glory.

It was at Perugia that things went very wrong indeed. A fixed odds betting scandal erupted in Italian football. Players were 'arranging' results, betting large sums of money and making still larger ones. Rossi was accused of being involved in a fixed 2–2 draw between his club and Avellino. He was alleged to have said casually, while playing cards, that he didn't care as long as he could score a couple of goals. He did, the game was drawn 2–2, and the unthinkable upshot was a three-year suspension for Rossi, later reduced on appeal to two years.

In the interim, he was transferred to Juventus, the very club which had discovered and rejected him. Without his inspiration, the Italian team struggled, though it did qualify for Spain, by which time Rossi was again allowed to play.

Taking Rossi to Spain was clearly a great risk. There had only been time for him to play three championship matches for Juventus and a handful of warm-up games with the Italian team. But Enzo Bearzot, the team manager who had launched him in Argentina, picked him. He had to gamble; the Italian attack had been hopelessly sterile all season.

At first, when the Italians opened their programme in Galicia, the gamble seemed doomed to failure. Rossi was as rusty as might have been expected. The old, darting opportunism seemed to have gone. Perhaps never to return. He looked far slower in thought, as well as movement. He was even substituted in the game against Peru.

By virtue of three undistinguished draws, Italy scraped into the second round in Barcelona, but there, too, at the Sarria stadium, Rossi made a poor beginning. True, Italy woke up admirably to beat Argentina in the opening game, but when Rossi was put clean through with only the goalkeeper, Fillol, to beat – the kind of chance he used to be able to put away almost in his sleep – he shot straight at the keeper and was lucky to see Conti return the ball into the centre for Cabrini to score.

Suddenly, in the second game against Brazil, everything came gloriously together. The Brazilians had been playing superlative football and were everybody's favourites to win, though ironically they badly lacked a centre-forward, a player to lead them in the superb tradition of Leonidas, Ademir, Vavà and their last fine leader, Tostão, who had been forced out of football with an eye injury. The Brazilian midfield, however, had been quite marvellous, they'd comfortably beaten Argentina and were expected to make a meal of Italy.

That was where Rossi came in. Single-handed, he exposed the two great weaknesses of the supposedly invincible Brazilian team: they hadn't got a decent centre-forward, and they hadn't got a decent defence. This quickly became plain when, after only five minutes, Rossi scored, thus proving how right Valdir Peres, the Brazilian keeper, had been when he said before the match that his chief fear was that Rossi might suddenly come to life.

Bruno Conti, the little Roma winger, sent the overlapping left-back, Antonio Cabrini, haring away down the left wing. Over came the cross, and a bemused Brazilian defence watched as Rossi stole in unsuspected and unhindered, to score one of his famous headed goals.

The beauty of it was that Italy, knowing that a draw would send Brazil through, had no alternative but to attack, though this was quite against the sadly sterile nature of their game.

At heart, however, the Italian is a natural attacking footballer whose true talent has been stifled – a fine ball-player with admirable ball skills who likes nothing better than to express himself, cut a fine figure, even play to the gallery.

The Brazilians equalized, but Rossi was irrepressible. To give the kind of ridiculous pass across his own penalty area which Cerezo, an exciting, attacking midfielder, gave was crazy with the likes of Rossi about. The ball never got to its intended recipient, the full-back Junior, for Rossi swooped and into the net it went. Italy 2, Brazil 1.

Brazil equalized again through a flashing shot by Falcão, a midfielder who played in Rome, but Rossi had yet another ace up his sleeve.

Fifteen minutes from the end, Brazil failed to clear a corner properly, Marco Tardelli banged the ball back into the goalmouth and when it broke to Rossi he was as deadly accurate as ever. Brazil were beaten 3–2 and Italy marched on at their expense.

In the semi-final against Poland, in the much bigger Nou Camp Stadium which belongs to the Barcelona club, Italy made short work of Poland, having drawn with them 0–0 in Vigo in their opening match. Again, Rossi scored the first goal with a very neat flick on the inside of his heel, exploiting a low free-kick and confusion in the goalmouth. His second goal, after half-time, was another of his characteristic headers, when he came running in unmarked on the far post, to convert Bruno Conti's fine centre from the left.

It seemed almost inevitable that Rossi would score in the Final in Madrid. So he did, thus breaking the deadlock early in the second half of what till then had been a boring, negative, ill-tempered game. This time, Tardelli quickly pushed a free-kick to Gentile on the right, two Italians missed his cross, but there once more was Paolo Rossi, running in from the left this time, to stoop low and score.

Silvio Piola was a very different centre-forward, but a very gifted one. He made an excellent debut in Vienna in March 1935, when the famous Peppino Meazza, a World Cup winner both in 1934 and 1938 (only Gioanin Ferrari, the inside-left, did as much) dropped out injured. In the second half, Piola, powerful, tall, with long, slender legs, scored two goals and was well and truly launched.

By the time the 1938 World Cup came round in France, Piola was so well established at centre-forward that Meazza had moved across to inside-right, as he'd been obliged to do before in 1934.

How close Piola and Italy came to going out in their very first match, against Norway in Marseilles!

Norway were then probably at their peak. They had a marvellous centre-forward called Brunyldsen, a Viking figure, whom Pozzo would, later, poetically refer to as 'a cruel thorn in my crown of roses'. They had an excellent left-winger called Per Brustad and they'd given a very strong Italian team of so-called students a hard run for their money in the Berlin Olympic soccer tournament two years before. The full-backs of that 'student' team, Foni and Rava, would keep their positions for the Italian national team in the 1938 World Cup Final.

Italy did get an early goal through Ferrari, in a move begun by Piola himself, but then R. Johansen, the Norwegian right-back, indicated Piola to Eriksen, his centre-half, who nodded his understanding. Piola, as a result, played little part in the game till Norway equalized in the second half. Suddenly he lost Eriksen, swooped on the ball when the goalkeeper blocked Paserati's shot, and gave Italy the goal which qualified them, by the skin of their teeth, for the second round.

Things were easier after that and Piola justified all the good things said about him before the competition.

He was on glorious form against France, the host country, at the Colombes Stadium. Adept with both feet and with his head, he not only scored goals but skilfully opened up the game for his colleagues. He had a lithe, explosive movement which would have been remarkable in an athlete, let alone in one as heavily built in the upper body as he. Gabriel Hanot, the French expert, said he recalled only one European forward who was his equal, and that was Six, a Belgium international who'd played in France for Lille, but sadly died in the Great War.

It was two fine second-half goals by Piola, when the score was 1–1, which cooked the French goose. A long ball from the clever Italian right-winger, Amedeo Biavati, famous for his double shuffle on the ball, split the French defence and allowed Piola the kind of clear run he always exploited.

For the third goal, Piola sent the other rapid Italian winger, Colaussi, down the left. Colaussi raced away, then booted the ball cross field to Biavati, the right-winger, who flicked it to Piola and he in turn headed past Di Lorto – a goalkeeper whose marvellous display had kept Italy at bay the last time they'd met France, earlier in the season.

Then came the semi-final against Brazil in Marseilles, where Piola found himself marked by the usually calm and polished Domingas

Da Guia, one of the best defenders in the world, a player who relied above all on positioning, technique and finesse and who would always rather win the ball by an interception, than a tackle. Much as Bobby Moore was to do years later.

Piola's aggressive, bustling methods, however, simply infuriated him. Colaussi gave Italy the lead, Piola raced away from Domingas half-a-dozen times and finally, untypically, Domingas lost his temper, hacked him down and, with Piola dramatically rolling over and over, found he had not only given away a penalty, but was banished from the field. Meazza scored from the spot and Italy were in the Final.

Would things have been vastly different if Tim and, above all, Leonidas of Brazil had played? The Black Diamond had played his one previous World Cup match four years earlier in Genoa, where Spain had promptly knocked out the Brazilians 3–1 and sent them straight home several thousand miles, after just ninety minutes' football.

Most observers felt that Leonidas would have snapped up the two chances missed by his deputy, Peracio, in Marseilles. Leonidas was only a little fellow, but his elasticity, his amazing overhead 'bicycle kick', his speed and courage, made him the terror of defences. His accuracy may be judged by the fact that in the three 1938 World Cup games he played he allegedly got every shot on target. Playing against Poland in the mud of Strasbourg – which might have been expected to cramp his style, but didn't – he took his boots off in the second half and threw them over the touch-line to his trainer, only to be told by Eklind, the Swedish referee, to put them on again.

Leonidas scored a hat trick in the first half and eventually came out of an astonishing game with four goals, the Brazilians winning after extra time by 6–5. Willimowski, the blond Polish inside-left, a dashing figure, scored four for Poland.

Back to Piola. In the Final against Hungary, he was again a tremendous force. After a qurter of an hour, with the score already 1–1, Hungary having immediately equalized Italy's sixth-minute goal by Colaussi, Piola scored from a pass by Meazza. Then with just ten minutes left he got the fourth Italian goal, thumping in a ball back-heeled to him by the flying Biavati. Italy won 4–2.

In the many tense, tight battles between Italy and Austria, one of which, in the World Cup semi-final of 1934 in Milan, enabled Italy to reach the Final, Mathias Sindelar was Austria's response to Meazza and Piola. You could scarcely find a player less like the robust Piola. Sindelar was so slim that he was nicknamed in Vienna 'the Man of Paper'. He relied on sheer skill, on wonderful control and an acute awareness of everything that was going on around him. He could, in the style of the elegant Vienna School of football, dribble round a whole defence, tricking them all including the goal-keeper, then simply walk the ball over the line. He led the Austrian attack when they beat France and their old foe Hungary in the first two rounds, but the heavy mud of Milan was not to his liking. It was far better suited to the ruthless Monti, the Argentine-born centre-half who once told Pozzo grimly, 'When I see Sindelar, I see red!' Many was the time Sindelar danced round Monti, especially in Vienna, but in Milan the combination of the mud and Monti's vigorous attentions blunted the edge of his delicate game.

Argentina themselves were famous for their centre-forwards. One of them, Guillermo Stabile, nicknamed 'the Infiltrator', was leading scorer of the first 1930 World Cup in Montevideo, where he scored eight goals, two in the semi-final against the heavy United States team made up largely of British players, and one against Uruguay, in a most exciting Final, a repeat of their keenly fought meetings in the Olympic Final, two years before.

In 1930, Stabile (who later, silver-haired, courteous and elegant, would go on to be team manager of Argentina) replaced Manuel Ferreira, the team's captain, in the second match, against Mexico. He scored three goals and kept his place. Ferreira, who had kept Stabile out of the opening game which had been very narrowly won against an excellent France, was taking his university examinations. Hardly the kind of reason you would hear today for missing a World Cup game.

So well did the elusive, incisive Stabile play that when Ferreira did come back, it was at inside-left.

As for Uruguay, they started with one of their most famous players, Petrone, at centre-forward, but he was well past his prime and they ended up, in the Final, with the one-armed Hector Castro, who played well and scored the final goal in the last seconds of the game. So Uruguay ran out winners, 4–2, of the first World Cup, having been given a great fright when they fell behind 2–1 to Stabile's goal, which they claimed was offside. Castro had taken the place of the injured Pelegrin Anselmo, a splendid young centre-forward who'd replaced Petrone after the first game and had scored three goals, but had then had the disappointment of missing a place in a winning World Cup Final.

The great Brazilian tradition of centre-forwards, as we have seen, continued after the war through Ademir, the less artistic but very forceful Vavà, a World Cup winner and scorer in 1958 and 1962, and Tostão, a medical student, saved for the 1970 World Cup by an eye operation in Houston, Texas, but forced to retire by 1974.

Tostão was a very different, less muscular, centre-forward than Vavà, a brave and thrusting player, adept at finishing off movements beautifully created by the likes of Garrincha and Zagalo, on the wings. When Sweden took the lead in the 1958 Cup Final in Stockholm, it was Vavà who zoomed in to bang home two passes pulled back from the line by Garrincha. Four years later, in the semi-final against Chile, the host country, it was Vavà again who headed in Garrincha's dropping corner and Zagalo's short centre. He wasn't a classic player, he hadn't the wonderful elusiveness of Leonidas and Ademir or the refined touch and the ability to play with his back to goal of Tostão, but how Brazil could have done with him in the World Cups of 1974, 1978 and 1982, when it became so clear that centre-forwards in that vast country did not, after all, grow on trees.

The Germans must have felt somewhat the same when Gerd Muller, having scored the winning goal in the 1974 World Cup Final against Holland, announced his retirement from international football.

To me Muller still seems one of the most phenomenal goal-scorers, both in and out of World Cups, of all time. When the likes of Piola and Leonidas were playing, defences were still fairly free and easy. The high fitness, the high organization, the close marking of the modern defence make goal scoring immeasurably harder. Yet the relatively short, thick-thighed Muller scored no fewer than sixty-nine goals in sixty-two internationals. What an astonishing variety of goals they were.

Some, like the goal which finally settled the 1970 quarter-final in hot, high León (Mexico), against England, were full-blooded, point-blank volleys. Some were the fruit of strong persistence, like the World Cup winner of 1974 when, after Bonhof had beaten Haan on the right flank and crossed, and Muller had had his first shot blocked, he spun, shot again and scored. Others were delicately lobbed headers. Somehow or other, he always managed to get himself into good scoring positions, despite the mass of defenders clustered thick around him.

Yet when it was first proposed that his club, Bayern Munich, should sign him, their manager, Zlatko Cjaicowski, right-half for Yugoslavia in the 1950 World Cup, was against it and had to be persuaded by the club's President. Muller rewarded them with a fusillade of goals, among them those which enabled Bayern Munich to win the European Cup Finals of 1974 and 1975. Untypically, he did not score in Glasgow when they beat Saint Etienne, in 1976.

In the 1970 World Cup, Helmut Schoen, West Germany's tall, gentle but persuasive manager, the man who transformed the German game adding subtlety to power and drive, put Muller side by side with Uwe Seeler, his famous predecessor as the German centre-forward. 'Uwe, Uwe, Uwe!' cried the crowds. It was a war cry and Seeler a warrior. To that extent, Seeler was more of a hero to the German crowd than Muller, who scored goals by stealth and who was often accused of 'only' doing that, rather than playing his part in the build up. To which all one can say is that if a centre-forward 'only' scores as many goals as Muller, some of which win World and European Cup Finals, then that centre-forward is priceless.

Uwe Seeler made his debut for West Germany just after the World Cup victory of 1954 against England at Wembley; most of the winning team had mysteriously gone down with jaundice which led to all sorts of dark murmurs (never substantiated) about stimulants. He would play in no fewer than four World Cups, a centre-forward in the old German battling-school style, following the effective but unexceptional Otmar Walter, whose brother Fritz was captain, inside-forward and guiding mind of the 1954 success.

Squarely built, robust and fearless, not very tall but excellent in the air, Seeler came back successfully even after an operation to give him an artificial Achilles tendon. He jumped superbly, shot strongly with his right foot and, as Jimmy McIlroy, an accomplished inside-right in Northern Ireland's 1958 World Cup team, once said, 'would go through a brick wall if he knew the ball was on the other side'.

Schoen, as we have seen, accommodated him in 1970 when Muller's star was rising by playing him most productively as an attacking inside-right. The two dovetailed very nicely and Seeler headed a remarkable goal with his back to the net against England, in that dramatic quarter-final tie.

If Muller was the supreme executioner of the West German 1974 World Cup winning side. Johan Cruyff was the masterly inspiration of the Dutch team beaten by Germany in the Final. Lankily built, enormously quick off the mark though he always said he was not very fast, inventive to a degree and a superb striker of the ball, Cruyff was, with Germany's sweeper Franz Beckenbauer, the greatest player of his day, not just in Europe but in the world.

His father died young, Cruyff joined Ajax of Amsterdam at the age of ten in one of their six junior teams and his mother used to scrub out the club's offices. As a centre-forward, he could never have played like Muller, nor would he have wanted to. He was, in the best sense, all over the place, now racing through the centre, now moving out to the left wing, now dropping behind his attack to pick up the ball and, with a beautifully judged pass, starting a new movement. He was not especially good in the air, nonetheless he did head a goal for Ajax against Internazionale of Milan in the European Cup Final of 1972.

In the World Cup of 1974, Cruyff was an incomparable dynamo, combining especially well with his Ajax and Barcelona colleague, Johan Neeskens; a powerful midfielder of great all-round talents. Perhaps Cruyff reached his considerable peak in the decisive second round game in the rain at Dortmund against Brazil, a game which put the team through to the Final.

Early in the second half Cruyff moved out to the right wing, received a ball from Neeskens, went on up the wing, judged his pass as perfectly as Neeskens did his run and then released a diagonal ball which Neeskens, at full pelt, sent looping over Leao, the keeper. Then Cruyff himself beautifully volleyed home a cross from the left wing by the superb attacking full-back, Rudi Krol, who by 1978 would be Holland's captain and sweeper.

In the Final, at the Munich Olympic Stadium, Cruyff got away in the very first minute, twisting and sprinting through the German defence, to be brought down in the box by Uli Hoeness. Neeskens scored from the penalty and everybody waited for the Dutch and Johan Cruyff to run riot. For some strange reason they didn't, though Cruyff still almost won the game for them late in the first half when he faultlessly held the ball, drew his man and sent Johnny Rep completely clear. Alas for Cruyff and Holland, Rep shot straight at Sepp Maier, the goalkeeper, and the Germans went on to win through Breitner's penalty and Muller's second-half goal.

Cruyff played on with Barcelona, but he wouldn't go to the 1978 World Cup Finals. A sad loss to Holland, and to the game.

3 The Managers

It may come as a shock to think that when England first entered the World Cup in 1950, they had only had a regular team manager for four years. The modern manager at both club and international level tends to be something of a star himself, forever giving interviews to radio and television, and receiving immense praise or blame, according to whether his team wins or loses.

Even so, the team manager was an important and popular figure in Europe long before the war. Vittorio Pozzo of Italy and Hugo Meisl of Austria were two excellent managers and were great friends as well as great rivals. They were highly educated, each speaking several languages, and tremendous admirers of English football. Indeed, they were both good friends of the famous Arsenal manager, Herbert Chapman, as original a manager in his own way, if not as intellectual, as they.

In fact, the year before the 1934 World Cup, when England played Italy for the first time ever in Rome, sturdy little Pozzo, with his brush of grey hair, came out of his dressing room and was most surprised to see Chapman, who had no official position, coming out of England's. When Pozzo asked him what he was up to Chapman replied, 'I'm doing the same thing for my team as you are doing for yours.' It was a 1–1 draw, the English goal being scored by the brilliant young Arsenal left-winger, Cliff Bastin.

Just before the 1934 finals, Hugo Meisl, who came from a wealthy Jewish Viennese family, told his goalkeeper–journalist brother Willy that his so-called 'wonder team' was too tired to win the Cup and that England would not even reach the semi-finals. But give me one English player, he went on, and we would still win the trophy. 'Who?' his brother asked. 'Bastin,' was the reply. But neither Bastin nor England took part in the 1934 World Cup and when England were asked to make up the number in France in

1938, after Hitler's Germany had swallowed up Austria, they refused. A pity, really, as their powerful team had just won in Germany and France.

Pozzo was born in Piedmont, a man of the mountains, and educated in Turin where the first centre-half of the very young, very amateur, Juventus team told him one day, 'You look so silly when you run, with nothing in front of you, like a motor car. Why don't you come and play with us? We run after a ball.' Pozzo joined them and eventually became one of the founders of the other Turin club, Torino. He first took over an Italian national team as early as 1912 when, at the last moment, he was asked to run the side which competed in the Olympic tournament in Stockholm.

Ironically enough, at a time when almost all the British clubs had gone over to the stopper centre-half and the third back game, Pozzo was using the old-school attacking centre-half and employing methods he had learned as a student in England before the Great War, when he had had long talks with such stars as Charlie Roberts, the attacking centre-half of Manchester United, and Steve Bloomer, the legendary, goal-scoring inside-right of Derby County, both of whom were English internationals. He wanted a centre-half like Roberts, who swung long balls to the wings, so he dropped the neat, elegant, ball-playing Fulvio Bernardini who, he felt, slowed down the side's play. Pozzo preferred to see the robust Luisito Monti, 'the Man Who Strolls', the tough Argentine whom we have already met, captaining his team to the Final of the 1930 World Cup.

He was proved right for again it was Monti who helped Italy win the 1934 World Cup Final against the Czechs, when two other Argentines, the wingers Guaita and Raimondo Orsi, figured in the team. 'If they can die for Italy, they can play for Italy,' Pozzo would say grandly, meaning that if a man, born abroad, could be called up as an Italian soldier, then he was eligible to be capped for Italy as a footballer. This phrase however took on an unfortunate irony when in 1936, after the Italians had invaded Abyssinia, several Argentine–Italian footballers were found trying to sneak across the Swiss borders to evade military service. One of them was Guaita.

'Kind, with a strong hand,' was Pozzo's motto. 'If I let them make mistakes, I would lose my authority.' He was a shrewd practical psychologist, up to all sorts of tricks, as he had to be with such temperamental players.

Sometimes, he would choose two players who had quarrelled in a League game and make them share the same room. Each in turn would approach him to complain, telling him that they had quarrelled. 'I know,' Pozzo would reply, 'but we are trying to build a team. You must convince yourself that this man is not an enemy but a friend.' The following morning, Pozzo would look into their room and ask, 'Well, cannibals? Have you eaten each other yet?' Each player would then approach him and say, 'You know, he's not really such a bad fellow. The crowd put me against him.'

Another favourite dodge of Pozzo's, when a headstrong player in a training game would not do as he was asked, was to sidle up to him a little later and say, 'You were right. I've been thinking. You *should* do so-and-so.' ('So-and-so' being exactly what Pozzo had wanted and the player hadn't!)

Above all, Pozzo built his teams on tremendous spirit, morale and commitment. In this, he was able to draw on the boisterous and rather unpleasant spirit of the times, for Italy was then a Fascist state under Mussolini, in which, as Cliff Bastin observed when he played in Rome, everybody seemed to wear a uniform and patriotic chants, parades and slogans were the order of the day. So Pozzo persuaded his men they were doing something for their nation and he, as an officer of the mountain regiment, the Alpini, became their general. A French journalist once called him 'the poor captain of a company of millionaires', and Pozzo thought this might well have been the secret of his success.

He was a stubbornly determined man. When he was studying in England and his family ordered him home he refused. He was too happy here. And when they cut off his allowance, he earned his keep by teaching languages throughout the Midlands.

He was lured home eventually to attend his sister's wedding though only with the help of a return ticket, but was then made to stay in Turin. He kept the return half of that ticket for the best part of fifty years.

Pozzo's teams, like Enzo Bearzot's in more recent years, could be very rough and rugged. Luisito Monti was the very model for the kind of player Pozzo preferred, though to be fair, he also used such beautifully accomplished, graceful footballers as Meazza. But the right-half-back, Ferraris IV, was a more typical Pozzo player, one who fought for every ball and was none too nice in his methods.

Similarly, Bearzot, a splendid, Red Indian figure, who once studied classics and whose father wanted him to be a doctor. He never hesitated to choose such players as Romeo Benetti and Claudio Gentile, each ferociously adept in the use of his elbows and each despite his undoubted skills a notoriously hard man. Gentile, indeed, so maltreated the brilliant Argentine inside-left, Diego Maradona, when Italy beat Argentina in Barcelona in 1982 that the shock waves are reverberating still, and if you criticized Benetti to Bearzot, his reply would be a sweet smile and the words, 'He's a canary breeder!' as if this explained and excused everything.

Pozzo badly wanted Ferraris IV – the fourth, that is, of a family of footballing brothers – for the 1934 World Cup, although he knew that he was smoking like a chimney and was far from fit. So he went down to Rome and spoke to him on the top step of the stadium's terraces.

'Do you think I can still do it?' asked Attilio Ferraris.

'Certainly,' said Pozzo, 'if you do what I tell you.'

'I'm smoking thirty to forty cigarettes a day,' admitted Ferraris; but then Gerson, the Brazilian inside-forward who played such a splendid game and scored such a marvellous left-footed goal against Italy in the Final of the 1970 World Cup, was said to have smoked sixty!

'We'll cut them down gradually,' said Pozzo.

'Let's try,' said Ferraris.

'Let's try,' said Pozzo.

They succeeded, and Ferraris won a World Cup medal. The sad sequel to it all, many years later, was that Ferraris took part in what the Italians called an Old Glories Game, during which he had a heart attack, collapsed and died.

Before the 1934 tournament began in Italy, Pozzo had another and still more serious problem to contend with. His brilliant new goalkeeper, the acrobatic Carlo Ceresoli of Inter, was out injured. He had been playing in a training game for the Italian team in Florence, indeed Pozzo had been leaning against the very goal post, when Ceresoli made a daring save and broke his arm in the process.

Giampiero Combi, the veteran Italian keeper, whose place had gone to Ceresoli, watched his unfortunate successor being taken to hospital, turned to Pozzo and said, 'Then it's up to me?' It was.

Otherwise, the only real problem the players came up against before the World Cup began was in the training quarters at Roveta, where the terrible din made by the peacocks prevented them going to sleep. 'Why did they ever save two of them for the Ark?' demanded the Bologna centre-forward, Schiavio, but evidently it had no permanent effect on him, since he eventually scored the winning goal in the World Cup Final.

Pozzo was not himself a Fascist, but he was, for all his pro-English feeling, a stern and dedicated patriot. In those nationalistic times it was customary for Italian teams to give the Fascist salute before every game. When this happened before the first match of the 1938 World Cup competition against Norway in Marseilles, hundreds of anti-Fascists, who had taken refuge in France where some, alas, were still brutally tracked down, burst into a storm of jeering. Pozzo told his players to drop their arms, then hold the salute until the jeering stopped, which it eventually did.

He always had a trick or two up his sleeve as he showed in Paris in the 1938 Final, when he was banned from coaching on the touchline.

The game was literally about to begin when two FIFA officials, one from Belgium, the other from Uruguay, came up on either side of him like a couple of coppers. 'Come with us,' they said, 'you'll be fine,' and took him to a seat well away from the touchline. There, he was told, he must stay until the game was over, with no coaching from the touchline!

Pozzo, however, wasn't easily beaten. By half-time he'd found a solution. Luisin Burlando, the team's coach, was told to lie at his feet and listen carefully while Pozzo mused aloud to himself in an obscure Italian dialect. Burlando, who of course understood every word, then sprang up and instructed the players. Once he was almost arrested by a *gendarme*, but he managed to talk his way out of it, and Italy, of course, went on to win.

Meisl was a less combative figure than Pozzo; more of a believer in pure football. The man who had helped him develop the fabled Vienna School game was of course Jimmy Hogan. But when Hogan first coached in Vienna before the First World War, he couldn't get his message across. He was dealing with university students, a very different audience from most of those he was used to (though he'd coached in Holland, too) and the session left him profoundly depressed. Something was wrong, but he didn't know what.

A long talk that night with the fluent, forceful Hugo Meisl soon put things right and from that time on, Hogan did wonderfully well in showing the Austrians, the Hungarians and the Germans exactly what he wanted. Indeed, when Hungary finally smashed England's unbeaten home record against foreign teams at Wembley in November 1953, the frail, grey-haired little Hogan was their guest of honour in the Royal Box. The principles of fine ball-control and short, subtle, intelligent passing – the classic Scottish game – had laid the foundation for the Central European game, too.

It was sad that Meisl and Hogan's Austria, with Sindelar, the resourceful attacking centre-half, Smistik, the hard-shooting inside-left, Schall, the clever right-winger and Zischek, should have played only one World Cup. They refused to go to Uruguay in 1930 and in 1938 their best players were filched to play for the so-called Greater German team.

Tough little Sepp Herberger was called in as their manager at the last moment after their disastrous 6–3 defeat by England and was still in charge when West Germany contested the Chilean World Cup of 1962. Meanwhile his team won the trophy in Switzerland in 1954, and took fourth place in Sweden in 1958.

I remember him being very amused by a report that he treated his players not like people but numbers. He was now going back, he said, with a smile, at the end of a Press Conference, to see numbers one, two and three!

There is no doubt that in his own, driving way, he was a very fine team manager, tactically shrewd and well able to take bold and successful decisions. Such as in 1954, for example, when at the very last moment he called the hefty Rot Weiss Essen winger, Helmut Rahn, back from a club tour of South America to play in the World Cup. With his strength, speed, dash and shot, Rahn was enormously effective and he ended gloriously by scoring two goals in the winning World Cup Final.

By 1958 Rahn was in a very bad way, overweight, seriously out of condition and living down the shame of a drunken driving charge. Herberger got hold of him, reinvigorated him and turned him once more into the immensely dangerous winger he had been in 1954. He had an extremely good World Cup in Sweden.

Herberger had his ideal captain in Switzerland in the clever Fritz Walter, an inside-forward who had been a paratrooper in the war and whose excellent ball control was allied to a keen tactical sense. Walter kept his team splendidly on the move and was a fine opportunist himself, not least in the semi-final when Austria were so surprisingly thrashed 6–1.

It was Herberger who craftily devised the plan for outflanking the great favourites Hungary, by willingly throwing away the first game 8–3, with a weakened team, in the well-justified hope that Germany would live to fight another day. Herberger was not averse to having skilful players in his team – Fritz Walter with his neat control was one of them – but he liked big, strong fighters best and when Uwe Seeler emerged in the mid-fifties, he had his ideal centre-forward too.

Himself an inside-forward once with Mannheim (his gentle successor, Helmut Schoen, had been an inside-forward with Dresden), Herberger was enormously practical and, despite his reputation, flexible. He could always adapt to any given situation, though it's doubtful whether he would have allowed Franz Beckenbauer and other gifted German players the freedom to play the so-called Total Football game. It even took Schoen three World Cups to let it happen.

Pozzo and Meisl were rather more than just team managers. Pozzo's official title was Commissario Tecnico, Technical Commissar, and he remained in office till 1948 when England beat Italy 4–0 in his native Turin. Later you would find him at World Cups as a journalist, long his profession, and I still treasure a picture of him roaming the night through the streets of Santiago like an unnoticed old lion whilst rapturous crowds celebrated Chile's third place in the tournament.

Enzo Bearzot, even had he wanted to, could never have been

the dominant, authoritarian figure Pozzo was. Times had changed. Italian players were just as temperamental, just as well paid, probably, in both cases, much more so, but the atmosphere was different. You could no longer wave Italian flags around and treat your players like soldiers. An often vicious and still more often meddlesome Italian Press could make life miserable for a manager, particularly one like Bearzot, a kind, sensitive man, easily hurt by cruel words and what he considered unfair treatment.

Not that Bearzot was a weak man, rather a passionate moralist of immense determination. Indeed his very involvement with football had required some courage, for when he first became a professional footballer, with Gorizia, rather than a medical student as expected, his bank manager father was dismayed and it was many years before Bearzot senior came to terms with his disappointment. 'Then,' says his son, 'he became a fan, but a silent one.'

As assistant coach in Germany in the 1974 World Cup, Bearzot was horrified by the behaviour in the Italian camp and deeply upset by accusations that the Italians had tried to bribe the Poles in their last and fatal match. In fact, he refused to speak to Italo Allodi, the then general manager of the 1974 World Cup side, ever again. Astonishingly, Allodi was later put in charge of the National Coaching Centre at Coverciano outside Florence, though he had no background in soccer coaching at all. He was an obscure footballer who made his way up on the administrative side and became secretary of Internazionale (Milan) in what have later been termed the Years of the Golden Fix. Inter were remarkably well treated by kind referees in their European Cup success of the period. Fulvio Bernardini, the former Italian international centre-half and team manager, remarked cuttingly that all Allodi knew was how to give gold watches to referees.

When Bearzot got his Italian team to Argentina and the so-called Hindu Club, for the World Cup of 1978, his players looked exhausted and sterile. Their last game before the competition had been a goal-less disaster and even key men such as midfielder Marco Tardelli seemed drained of vitality.

Bearzot had to create an atmosphere of tranquillity and optimism to purge the players of their tension and anxiety. He succeeded splendidly, not least by keeping the mischievous journalists out of the training camp except at specified morning Press Conferences. Tardelli was one of those who blossomed in the peace of the Hindu Club like some previously wilting flower; he had an excellent World Cup. For Bearzot *l'ultimo traguardo*, as he put it, the final objective, was Total Football. He wanted to bring Italian football out of the pathetic, negative, defensive crouch in which it had been hiding for so many years, years which included the humiliating defeat by North Korea at Middlesbrough in the 1966 World Cup and the thrashing by Brazil in the 1970 Final, and put it back on the international soccer map.

He succeeded admirably, partly because France scored a goal in less than thirty seconds at Mar del Plata, forcing the Italians to come out and attack. They won 2–1.

The journalists, who would be banned and banished completely in the 1982 tournament by the exasperated players, seriously overstepped the mark one morning at the Hindu Club. They did not get away with it. When the players were a little late in coming down the Press made an awful fuss, much to the embarrassment of the courteous Bearzot, who excused himself saying, 'I can't take them by the neck and drag them down.' Eventually the players did appear and gave long and amiable interviews to the usual groups of journalists, but the following morning when the journalists made the twenty-mile trip out to the club, there was no one there at all. Even Bearzot himself was only to be seen behind plate glass, in the unattainable gardens of the Club. Furious, the journalists had to return to Buenos Aires empty handed and with empty notebooks.

In the end Italy took fourth place but until they eventually ran out of steam in the second round, they acquitted themselves well and, despite the bitter opposition from Allodi and certain of Allodi's journalist friends, Bearzot was confirmed as manager for another four years. Again, he was subjected to often spiteful criticism, not least because he refused to make whole-scale changes in his team. As if to prove his point, he managed to qualify them again for the World Cup, but when the team began so badly in the opening round's matches in Galicia, criticism again became violent especially from Coverciano, where Allodi was presiding over a conference of club managers.

One of them, the manager of the Varese club near Milan, particularly incensed Bearzot by stating that all Italian managers should publicly disassociate themselves from Bearzot and his tactics.

Italy qualified, however, and on the plane to Barcelona for the second round Federico Sordillo, the new President of the Italian Football Federation, told Bearzot that whatever happened in the second round (there seemed not a hope of his winning the World Cup) he would be asked to stay on as manager for yet another four years.

To this, Bearzot replied that he certainly wouldn't stay on if he were still to have an enemy at his back. Italy did, as we know, win the World Cup, Bearzot stayed on and Allodi was forced out of Coverciano. Typically, he immediately picked up a still better paid job as Chief Executive of the nearby Fiorentina (Florence) club. Such was the nature of Italian football.

Little George Raynor, a Yorkshireman from the village of Hoyland, suffered similar experiences in his one short, hectic season in Italy as manager of Juventus and Lazio in 1954/5. But he will always be remembered best for the marvellous job he did as manager of Sweden, where he was aptly described as 'a good manager for a happy team'.

He won the London Olympic tournament of 1948 with splendid players such as the three Nordahl brothers, Gunnar Gren 'the Professor' at inside-right, and Nils Liedholm, who managed Roma to their first Italian Championship since 1942 in 1982/3. But almost as soon as the Olympics were over, Italian and Spanish clubs swooped and Raynor lost nearly all his stars. He was still able and resilient enough to build a new team which not only qualified for the World Cup in Brazil in 1950, but was good enough to take third place.

It was all a very far cry from Raynor's obscure days as what he admits was 'only a second-class footballer', an outside-right with Rotherham (where he had to drive a coal lorry in the summer to make ends meet) and Aldershot.

The war was the making of him. He found himself coaching in Iraq where his good work was noticed by Stanley Rous, then the Football Association secretary and later, from 1962 to 1974, the President of FIFA.

After the war, when Raynor was only second-team trainer at Aldershot, a kind of magic F.A. carpet whisked him away to Sweden as national team manager. Perhaps it was not surprising that when he got there in 1946 he met hostility at first. Birmingham City were on tour in Sweden and when local journalists asked them about Raynor they said they had never heard of him.

But it didn't take the bubbling Raynor very long to win everybody round. In their first match Sweden were due to play Switzerland who were puzzling people at the time with their so-called bolt or *catenaccio* (Italian for 'great big chain') system, which featured a *libero*, or sweeper, operating behind the usual last line of defence. Using one of the Nordahl brothers, Knud (a full-back who was to play centre-half in the 1950 World Cup), at inside-forward, Raynor worked out a strategy to beat this bolt system. He told the journalists what he meant to do and why. Sweden won easily and Raynor was launched.

When it came to the 1950 World Cup, he made fine use of a Swedish custom known as 'Tomorrow's Men', training camps for promising young players. Out of this system, at a time when good inside-forwards were so rare in Europe, he produced two brilliant young players, Kalle Palmer of Malmo and Lennart 'Nacka' Skoglund of A.I.K. Stockholm, which he had joined from Third Division football only at the end of 1949. Later Skoglund was to make a brilliant name for himself at inside- and outside-left in Milan with Internazionale and on the left-wing for Sweden in the 1958 World Cup.

To return to 1950, Gunnar Nordahl, the massive centre-forward, had gone off to form the so-called 'GRENOLI' trio for Milan with Gren and Liedholm, but Raynor found a replacement for him in the tall, powerful Hans Jeppson whom he had often coached in his travels round Sweden. Jeppson liked to say he could only score goals and indeed he got a couple when the holders, Italy, were beaten and surprised 3–2 in São Paolo in their opening game. But in fact his distribution was useful too and he had a short, excellent spell early in 1951 when Charlton Athletic were a First Division club in South East London.

Before the tournament opened, Sweden played a practice game against a Rio club, in which Palmer and Skoglund wove all kinds of pretty patterns and left the field thoroughly pleased with themselves. Raynor gave them a stern telling off, informing them that this kind of football led nowhere and they had better not try it against the Italians. Nor did they.

By 1958 Sweden had accepted professionalism. This not only meant that certain stars such as Gren returned to Sweden, but that others playing abroad, such as Skoglund, Liedholm and Kurre Hamrin, who had been playing marvellously at outside-right for Fiorentina, were also able to return to represent their country.

As you can imagine it was a pretty old team, with some of its players, such as Gren and Liedholm, nearer forty than thirty. 'We're the slowest team in the competition,' said Raynor cheerfully, after Sweden had beaten Hungary 2–1 in Stockholm. 'If there was a relay race between all the teams, Sweden would finish last. But we'll still reach the Final!'

In this he was right, but he was wrong in a later forecast: 'If the Brazilians give away an early goal they panic all over the show.' Sweden did get an early goal, beautifully scored by Nils Liedholm who picked his way through a penalty area crowded with large, tough defenders. But Brazil were 2–1 ahead by half-time and they ran out the winners, 5–2.

If Raynor was a protégé of Sir Stanley Rous, Walter Winterbottom, England's team manager from 1946 to 1962, was even more of one. He was Raynor's exact opposite: a tall, rather schoolmasterly man, who had played a few pre-war games for Manchester United, studied physical education at Carnegie College and achieved high rank in the Air Force during the war. Quite how this qualified him to be manager of the England team is still not wholly clear, but obviously Rous felt it did. Fluent and dedicated, Winterbottom combined this task, which was later to earn Bobby Robson £70,000 a year and cause him to give up managing Ipswich Town, with that of Director of F.A. Coaching. Significantly, Winterbottom always considered the latter the more important job.

Raynor, like managers such as Sepp Herberger of Germany, had something of the guerrilla general about him. Herberger was not a club manager; Raynor was never very happy trying to be one. By the same token, Helmut Schoen and Jupp Derwall, Herberger's West German successors, came up through the official coaching system, and Bearzot had only one brief spell in club management, running the little Prato team.

Winterbottom, neither guerrilla general nor club manager, was a likeable, eloquent man of great presence. He loved weaving theories about the game, but didn't find it quite so easy to put them across to hardened professionals. He was often compromised by the selection committee which picked his teams for him, and he showed little grasp of tactics. Despite this, his World Cup record was an honourable one, even if on the first two occasions it was vastly easier for England to qualify than it is now; the British Championship, as we have seen, led a double life, as a qualifying group.

Once when the England team was in training at Roehampton on the Bank of England ground, Winterbottom told his forwards to run down the field, inter-passing, then put the ball into the empty net. Len Shackleton, a wonderfully gifted, very strong-willed inside-forward, looked up at him wearily, 'Which side of the goal, Mr Winterbottom?'

Job security – the knowledge that your position is safe and sound whatever happens – is something most club and international managers envy and there are those, like Pozzo, Bearzot, Herberger and Schoen, who served long periods at the helm of their national team. But Winterbottom was more like a permanent civil servant in some ministry. Governments could fall, teams could lose and alter, but Winterbottom would remain unchanged and unchallenged.

It is hard to think of any other footballing country in the world where he could have stayed in office after England's sensational 1–0 defeat by the United States in Belo Horizonte, Brazil, in 1950, but stay he did. Sir Stanley Rous never wavered in his championship of him, and his team, with their easy qualification system, never failed to reach the final stages of the World Cup competition, and even made the quarter-finals in 1954, 1958 and 1962. It was left to his very different successor, Alf Ramsey, to actually win the tournament.

'We shall win the World Cup,' said Ramsey, as soon as he was appointed, in 1962. He came from a poor family in Dagenham, Essex, which in 1920 was the London over-spill town; many East

Londoners had moved there before the war. His early ambition was to be a grocer and he came to football curiously late, first for Southampton during the war as an inside-forward, then as a particularly fine right-back, the position he played in the World Cup finals of 1950, in Brazil.

You do not find his type of full-back today – he would be considered altogether too slow and immobile – but in those days he was a highly original and influential player. At Tottenham Hotspur, where he moved in the summer of 1949, he was nicknamed 'the General' because of his influence over the team. He was a superb user of the ball and made a tremendous impact on that famous 'push and run' side, which operated under the slogan of its manager, Arthur Rowe: 'Make it simple, make it accurate, make it quick.'

Soon after retiring as a player Ramsey became manager of Ipswich Town, then a modest little Third Division club, founded and run by the powerful, East Anglian Cobbold family. He took them into Division Two, then won the Second and First Division Championships in successive seasons, building a fine team out of unexceptional players whom he used with enormous tactical skill.

He made a poor beginning with England, losing the first Nations Cup match 5–2 away to France in Paris, but he always knew he had one colossal advantage over Winterbottom. The tournament was going to be played in England.

Ramsey's style of football displeased many people, to whom he seemed too cautious and defensive, unwilling to countenance unorthodox, eccentric players like Jimmy Greaves – the little London goalscorer who would eventually, to his bitter regret, be left out of the 1966 World Cup Final.

There was also the question of wingers. When Ramsey took over the team he used them and was still using them right into the first games of the 1966 World Cup. Then he threw them out, going over to what amounted to a 4-4-2 system, with Alan Ball, the Blackpool inside-forward, and Martin Peters, the West Ham right-half, operating deep on the right and left flanks, respectively. Unfortunately this was to have profound and highly negative effect on the development of the English game, in which for years the emphasis would be placed on physical fitness and hard running, with wingers being so discouraged and unfashionable that schoolboys gave up their ambitions to be one.

Whether Ramsey reached this policy by design is hard to say. On occasion he would insist that not having wingers was a matter of policy, that he felt they were out of date. At other times he would say the only reason he left them out was because there weren't any really good ones at the time of the 1966 tournament.

What is true beyond doubt is that Ramsey could 'motivate' his teams in a way Winterbottom never could. With his expressed belief that football was something of greater importance than mere sport and his open contempt for those outside the magic playing and managerial circle, including selectors (who were now reduced to mere committee members) and journalists, he won the hearts of his players, who felt he cared for them: though some would change their minds bitterly in years to come, when they lost their places in the team.

Like Pozzo and Bearzot, Ramsey had a liking for hard men. There was toothless little Nobby Stiles of Manchester United, a ferocious tackler (though not much of a passer) and leech-like right-half, who could always mark any given player out of the game. After the 1966 World Cup game against France at Wembley when Stiles had committed an especially ferocious tackle on Jacky Simon, the F.A. Secretary, Denis Follows, amongst others, insisted that Stiles be dropped. Ramsey was furious and said that if Stiles was dropped, he would resign. They both stayed and after the World Cup Final a tearful Stiles approached Ramsey: 'You did it, Alf!' he sobbed. 'We'd have been nothing without you.' That may well have been so. Ramsey truly built a team, as Pozzo once did, and his words to his exhausted, disappointed players, as they lolled on Wembley's turf waiting for extra time, were characteristic: 'You've won it once; now you must win it again.'

Beneath Ramsey's apparently stony exterior, however, strong emotions bubbled. This was clearly shown at Wembley after the 1966 quarter-final in which the Argentine players had not only played with cynical, calculated thuggery, as a result of which their captain, Antonio Rattin, was sent off, but had behaved disgracefully afterwards in the dressing-room corridor. A seething Ramsey, interviewed for television shortly after the game, said that he felt that in the semi-final England would play its best against a team interested in playing football, and 'not act as animals'. That little phrase was to haunt him in an outraged Latin America for the rest of his England career.

And not least in Mexico, where he took the England team to defend their title in 1970. The previous year, Ramsey had brought his England team to Mexico City in the hope of winning friends and influencing people, but his notorious dislike of foreigners and foreign ways proved too strong for him.

Immediately after the match in Mexico City, a goal-less draw in which England suffered badly from the high altitude of over seven thousand feet, Ramsey gave a short Press interview. He was asked whether there was anything he'd like to say to the Mexican journalists. 'Yes,' he replied crisply, 'there was a band playing outside our hotel, at five o'clock this morning. We were promised a motorcycle escort to the ground. It never arrived. When our players went out to inspect the pitch, they were abused and jeered by the crowd. I should have thought the Mexican public would have been delighted to welcome England. Then when the game began, they could cheer their own team as much as they liked. But' (suddenly remembering his desire to make friends) 'we are delighted to be in Mexico, and the Mexican people are a wonderful people.'

The bird came home to roost the next year when the Mexican Press, furious at various snubs from Ramsey, conducted a spiteful campaign against him and the English team. It reached its peak the night before England were due to play a vital noonday match in the city of Guadalajara against Brazil. The Hilton Hotel where they were staying was besieged by hundreds of Brazil-favouring Mexican fans. They roared round the hotel on motorcycles, sang and shouted and occasionally tried to invade the hotel till two in the morning, while the England players had to change their rooms and move to the other, quieter side of the hotel. The police did stop the fans from actually breaking into the hotel, but that was as far as they went. They made no attempt to break up the rowdy demonstration, with which they appeared to be in sympathy. Ramsey had made no friends in Mexico.

Yet he did well with the team there, and if his marvellous goalkeeper, Gordon Banks, had not fallen ill after drinking a bad bottle of beer in León, England would probably have beaten West Germany in the quarter-final, instead of losing 3–2 after holding a two-goal lead. But Ramsey still has to take some blame for the defeat. This was the first World Cup in which substitutes were allowed and he never really learned how to use them.

When England were winning 2–1, and his attacking full-backs were clearly exhausted in the heat, he foolishly left them on but took off Bobby Charlton who had been dominating the midfield. Franz Beckenbauer, who had been marking Charlton, and who had scored the West German goal with a shot which slid under poor Peter Bonetti's diving body, was thus given time, space and a chance to move forward. In the meantime the German substitute, right-winger Jurgen Grabowski, ran rings round a now exhausted left-back, Terry Cooper.

Time ran out for Ramsey early in 1974, after England had been eliminated from the World Cup in Germany by Poland. He'd obviously shot his bolt long before, as managers alas do, and was becoming more and more defensive, and less and less adventurous. But his contribution to England's fine performance in two World Cups had been immense.

Scotland's Jock Stein was a remarkable manager of Celtic, the Glasgow club which in 1967 became the first British club ever to win the European Cup. Unfortunately, by 1982, when he took Scotland to Spain, he was past his peak, partly as a result of an appalling motor accident on his way back from Glasgow Airport.

Little Northern Ireland threw up two interesting managers in Peter Doherty, who against all odds got the team to Sweden in 1958 where it acquitted itself well, and Billy Bingham, the Irish right-winger in Sweden, who as manager took his Northern Ireland team to its distinguished performance in Spain in 1982.

Peter Doherty had been a great inside-left, a rangy, red-headed player who was practising Total Football long before anybody had ever heard of the term. He was something of a stormy petrel, very dissatisfied with the way professional footballers were treated and most displeased that the Ireland teams in which he played were given second-class status, their players often held back by English clubs and only thrown together as a side at the very last moment. But under his control, Northern Ireland developed a new pride in themselves and his managership coincided with a sudden flowering of fine players: the Blanchflower brothers, Jimmy McIlroy at inside-forward, Harry Gregg in goal, tough, tiny Wilbur Cush at inside-forward or even Bingham himself at outside-right.

When Northern Ireland and Italy were drawn in the same qualifying group, it seemed unthinkable that the Irish would survive, but survive they did, deservedly beating the Italians in Belfast 2–1, after unluckily losing 1–0 in Rome when the full-back Sergio Cervato cunningly and illegally moved the ball, before driving home a free-kick.

As his lieutenant, what the Italians would call his manager on the field, Doherty had the elegant, strong-minded right-half Danny Blanchflower who, like Doherty, had his own firm ideas about the way footballers were treated. He had a great sense of humour and before the 1958 World Cup announced that the Irish plan was to equalize before the other team had scored!

Years later in West Germany, something of the same relationship existed between Johan Cruyff and Rinus Michels who managed Cruyff at Ajax, Amsterdam and at Barcelona. Rinus Michels took over a brilliant, undisciplined, money-mad Dutch team just before the 1974 tournament, and just in time. It was under his management that Ajax's Total Football had reached its peak, dominating Europe and in no time at all he had his many former Ajax players and their colleagues happily organized and eager to win. They very nearly did. Michels was a forceful, authoritative figure and he certainly needed to be with so many temperamental and irascible players to keep contented.

Four years later, the Dutch manager was the melancholy, controversial Austrian, Ernst Happel, little liked by his players, but nonetheless capable of taking them to the Final. He'd been an excellent full-back and stopper in the fine Austrian team of the early 1950s, which first played the old Vienna School tactics of an attacking centre-half, then switched to the stopper third back and the W formation for the 1954 World Cup. Happel played in four of the games, including the amazing quarter-final in Lausanne where Austria beat Switzerland 7–5 and the disastrous semi-final in Basel where Germany beat Austria 6–1, but he missed the third place match when Austria beat Uruguay 3–1.

In later years, he would have great success at both club and international level, eventually winning the European Cup with Hamburg in 1983. He could so easily have won the 1978 World Cup too; indeed, had a shot by the Dutch left-winger, Rob Rensenbrink, in the last minutes of ordinary time in the Final against Argentina gone in, instead of hitting the post, he – and Holland – would have won.

Instead the World Cup went to Argentina and their manager, the chain-smoking Cesar Luis Menotti. Menotti had taken over the national team after its failure in the 1974 World Cup, when it reached the second round in West Germany, but was then no match for the Dutch, whom they would meet again in the 1978 Final.

Nicknamed 'El Flaco', the Thin One, a talented right-half with a powerful shot who had played not only in Buenos Aires but for Santos, Pelé's club, in Brazil and for the short-lived Generals in New York, Menotti boldly embraced a new policy.

For decades Argentine football had been poised between thuggery and skill. Sometimes you found both together, even in the same player; brilliantly talented footballers who could also commit savage fouls.

Since 1958, when Argentina sent a slow, elderly team, much weakened by the raids of Italian clubs, to Sweden and lost humiliatingly 6–1 to Czechoslovakia, the emphasis had been on muscle rather than skill. There was great envy of the Brazilians, who for many years had been regarded as inferior footballers, jeered at for their many black players, but who had now become a dominant team.

Argentine violence reached an alarming peak in the late 1960s when their teams started winning the so-called Liberators' Cup, the South American equivalent of the European Cup for clubs, and their 1966 World Cup side, as we have seen, made a dreadful impression in England.

Argentine teams were involved in some horrifying episodes especially in the Intercontinental Cup, the alleged world championship for clubs, played on a home-and-away basis by the winners of the European and the Liberators' Cup. Manchester United, Celtic and Milan all received scandalous treatment in South America, being kicked, punched, spat on, elbowed in the face and generally intimidated.

Menotti at once said he wanted none of it. 'If I thought such methods could win Argentina the 1978 World Cup', he said, 'I'd use them; but they couldn't.' The door was thus thrown open to the highly skilled players who have always abounded in Argentine football, though the leopard hadn't wholly changed its spots. In Buenos Aires in 1977, when a disappointing series of preparatory games was played, Argentine players committed disgraceful fouls on both English and Scottish players, and in the World Cup itself Daniel Passarella, the versatile, mobile centre-half, a scorer as well as a preventer of goals, distinguished himself by the malign use of his elbows. Indeed, in the first half of the World Cup Final, he made for himself no fewer than four headed chances to score and later smashed Neeskens of Holland to the ground with his elbow.

Nevertheless, Menotti, by and large, did prefer players with skill to those who would merely do physical damage to the opposition and much to his credit he did encourage his 1978 team always to attack, to take the initiative, to go for goals.

Argentina's eventual victory was, it is true, a badly flawed one. Referees had blatantly favoured them, not least in the Final itself, appallingly officiated by the Italian, Gonella. Nor is it easy to forgive him for the deeply displeasing events before the match began. Incredibly, in a game about to be watched not only by a huge crowd but by the best part of a billion television spectators, Argentina were five minutes late coming on to the field.

When they did get there, they immediately protested about a very light bandage worn by the Dutch winger, René Van de Kerkhof, round his forearm, a bandage which could not possibly have done anybody any harm, unlike the elbows of the protesting captain, Passarella. Van de Kerkhof, whose twin brother was in the Dutch midfield, eventually went off to change the bandage, but bitter feelings remained. Later in the summer, when the River Plate club of Buenos Aires and the P.S.V. club of Holland played in the same tournament in Spain – Van de Kerkhof and Passarella being present – the Dutch players would not speak to the Argentines.

There was also, of course, the little matter of Argentina's dubious 6–1 victory over Peru. On the whole, Menotti has always talked a fairer game than he has played, but there is no doubt he had a very positive effect on the 1978 team.

The following year he actually went to Tokyo with the Argentine youth team that won the world tournament and was welcomed in the streets of an ecstatic Buenos Aires by five million supporters! The phenomenal inside-left Diego Maradona, first capped for Argentina at sixteen, but dropped by Menotti from the 1978 World Cup squad as a seventeen-year-old, played in that team.

In 1982 the Argentines hoped that the combination of Menotti and a now more mature, twenty-one-year-old Maradona, with his thick-thighed strength, his glorious skill, his pace off the mark and his flair for the unexpected, would be good enough to retain the Cup. But apart from one fine performance against Hungary, Maradona had a poor World Cup, which ended with his being sent off for a bad foul on the Brazilian Batista in Barcelona. Oddly enough Batista had been the victim, four years earlier in Rosario, of a still worse foul by Ricky Villa, the Argentine inside-left, who a few months later would join Tottenham, and score a wonderful winning goal in the Cup Final.

In the game against Italy in Barcelona, there's no doubt that Maradona was disgracefully maltreated by Claudio Gentile, his Italian marker, but Italian reporters sharply criticized Menotti for playing Maradona so far up the front, virtually as a striker rather than a midfielder, thus enabling Gentile to mark him (almost literally) out of the game.

That Menotti's view of Maradona, like Bearzot's view of Gentile, is a rather special one was shown when, almost a year later, he said in Barcelona that Maradona was one of the purest footballers he had ever seen, one who never created problems for a referee, never retaliated after a foul. There were some who felt that the incident with Batista was a question of six of one, half a dozen of the other, that each had raised his studs at the same time, but to see Maradona as a kind of young saint seemed to be stretching the truth somewhat far.

How much, though, can a manager really do? As Maradona himself has said, 'Menotti may be a phenomenon, but if after we go on the field we don't bring off everything we've worked on with him through the week, he can't work miracles from the bench.'

The idea of the all-conquering, all-seeing manager, a kind of demi-god, is comparatively new in British football. Walter Winterbottom, as we have seen, lasted sixteen years, yet didn't come into that category at all, and before the war, before they ever had a manager, the England team record against foreign opposition – often with high-powered managers – was very respectable. They never lost a game at home and they won a good many away.

In some ways I think it rather unhealthy that a manager should be considered so crucially important; but he was important on the Continent as early as the days of Pozzo and Meisl in the 1920s. I think Nobby Stiles was right in thinking that England would never have won the 1966 World Cup without the inspiration of Alf Ramsey. I think Bearzot, in a very different, less authoritarian way than Pozzo, made it possible for Italy to do well in 1978 and to win in 1982, largely by creating the right, quiet conditions for his teams, and by encouraging them to play good, attacking football. But without him they tended to fall apart, as they did instantly after their triumph in Spain. They then played a string of disastrous games in the European Nations Cup, losing embarrassingly both to Rumania and Sweden and failing even to win their home games. It was a far cry from the days of Pozzo, who could crack the whip when he wanted.

At their best, managers clearly do two things. Or rather some managers do, some do only one of two things. The first is to create the kind of confidence, the high morale, on which winning teams are founded. The other, which is obviously closely connected but does not always necessarily follow it, is to plan winning teams and tactics. You do not have to be as dourly determined as a Ramsey, or as commanding as a Pozzo, to create a confident team. You can be a jolly little man like George Raynor, who made his players like him, and planned his tactics cleverly.

To use Brazil as an example. In 1970, under the skilled leadership of Mario Lobo Zagalo, deep-lying outside-left in the World Cup winning teams of 1958 and 1962, who was appointed only in March 1970 after his predecessor, João Saldanha, had quarrelled with Pelé and been booted out, Brazil won the World Cup and won it gloriously. Zagalo had managed to pull the team together, restore morale and pick a team in which both his left-footed schemers, Gerson and Rivelino, could find a role. For this he must be given credit. But good management alone cannot produce winners; thus in 1974, lacking players of sufficient calibre, all even Zagalo could offer in West Germany was a bleak, sour, defensive team which was rapidly eliminated by the Dutch.

At the other end of the scale, a manager can have a severely negative effect. Take Claudio Coutinho, Zagalo's immediate successor. As an Army officer who had initially been in charge of physical training, he wanted his team to play what he considered to be 'European' football, which in his book meant fine physical condition, an emphasis on hard running, tackling and chasing back. The Brazilians hated it. They were essentially artists, jugglers, even exhibitionists. Zico, the fine little inside-left, quarrelled with Coutinho. Though it so nearly reached the Final, the team looked uneasy and uninspired. Then along came a new manager, Tele Santana, and the trend was reversed. Talent was again encouraged and although there was still a mysterious lack of great forwards, a marvellous midfield of Zico, Socrates, Falcão and Toninho Cerezo played beautifully in Spain.

The trouble is the more important managers become, the more players tend to rely on them. Before the war England teams consisted of experienced professionals who never felt the need of long tactical talks or detailed instructions. They went out on the field, sized up the situation and used their initiative.

Indeed, although the coach is now a commonplace in Britain, there is still a basic mistrust of and hostility towards the idea of coaching, which is felt to be strictly for foreigners. This may have been true in the old days, when the game was developing abroad, but there is always a place for good coaching, whether it be in improving a player's skills or devising sensible tactics. The trouble is there are always more bad coaches than good and, sadly, the modern tendency is towards caution, defensive play, safety first: as England showed in their World Cup game against West Germany in Madrid, terrified lest right-back Manny Kaltz get in his crosses!

Walter Winterbottom used to say that a great international team could only be built around a nucleus of three or four great players.

That is still true. When you have such players, you don't really need a dominating manager, he should simply keep out of the way and let them get on with it, as the Hungarians did in the 1950s and the Brazilians later on.

It was, after all, Paolo Rossi who won the 1982 World Cup for Italy, Mario Kempes who won it in 1978 for Argentina and Pelé who did so much to win it in 1958 and 1970 for Brazil.

4 Shocks and Surprises

One thing the World Cup has almost unfailingly done is throw up shocks and surprises. With the exception of the early tournaments of 1934 and 1938, it has not been a straightforward knock-out competition, hence major upsets are less likely, but there have been nevertheless surprises galore.

The greatest of these was surely when in 1950 the United States of America defeated England 1–0 in the Brazilian city of Belo Horizonte.

On the face of it, it should have been a one-horse race. True, it was not the Americans' first venture into a World Cup. They had entered the 1930 competition and given a surprisingly good account of themselves, but at that time their team had been built round a core of British professionals – men who had stayed in the States after an attempt to get the professional game going there in the 1920s had fizzled out.

The 1930 American team was made up, for the most part, of big, hefty fellows, whom the amused French team nicknamed the Shot Putters after watching them toil around the track in training. But they were not to be sneered at on the field. They actually beat a far from weak Belgian team 3–0, then won against Paraguay, by the same convincing score. Patenaude, the centre-forward, scored all three goals.

In the semi-final against Argentina they were not quite good enough, as we know, and lost 6–1. But they were also responsible for one of the funniest incidents of the competition when their trainer ran on to protest to John Langenus, the famous Belgian referee, dropped his box of medicaments and was overcome by the fumes of a broken bottle of chloroform.

This 1930 team was perhaps the best international side the United States has ever produced. Marcel Pinel, the French centre-half, said of them, 'They played with the three forwards up and the rest of the team solidly massed in defence. They were immensely strong and tremendously fit and fast. Half a dozen breakaways in a game and they scored their goals.' Modern football, indeed.

The 1950 team may not have been as good, but it was not to be despised either. Interestingly, several of its finest players were born in America. The left-wing pair of John and Ed Souza (unrelated) came from the Fall River area in New England which had produced any number of talented footballers. This in sharp contrast with today, when ignorant but self-important college coaches control the game. Profoundly influenced by a background in American sport, in which the principles and practices of the native gridiron game bulk large, they produce little more than big, strong, over-trained, untalented musclemen, with little skill and only a minimal basic awareness of the game. Pro. soccer had come back to the States in 1967, when two professional leagues were formed, but ironically the truly gifted, good American players were all to be found in previous years.

Like the 1930 American team the 1950 team was captained by a British professional, Eddie McIlvenny, a fair-haired right-half who had been given a free transfer by the Third Division club, Wrexham. There were also a couple of other foreigners in the team, Maca, a Belgian born left-back and Larry Gaetjens, a Haitian who would score the winning goal and who would later sadly and mysteriously disappear.

The Americans did surprisingly well against Spain in their opening match in Curitiba. John Souza, who played splendidly throughout, gave them the lead before half-time, but in the second half the Spaniards hit back with three goals.

Still, they seemed to stand little chance against a strong England side which had just beaten Chile 2–0 in Rio and had marvellous players such as Stanley Mortensen, the goal-scoring inside-right of terrific shot and speed, Wilf Mannion of Middlesbrough, a blond, quick, brilliant inside-left and Tom Finney, one of the best and cleverest wingers in the world, so good that he was keeping out even the legendary Stanley Matthews. With hindsight, people say Matthews should have played and no doubt his elusive, sinuous dribbling and his famous swerve outside the full-back would have puzzled Maca. But on the face of it, the England team looked strong enough to beat a team far more powerful than America.

The Americans were certainly a lot tighter and tougher than they had been in the disastrous Olympic tournament of 1948 in London, when they played with an old-fashioned roving centre-half, and were smashed 9–0 by Italy. By 1950 four members of that team, plus a reserve, had gone to Brazil, which suggests that the Americans were no more concerned about the niceties of amateurism than were the Italians or many others. They also had a very good, lively manager.

Bill Jeffrey was a little Scotsman who went to the United States in the 1920s, worked on the railway, and played for his works team. One day he played for them against the Penn State College team in Pennsylvania. They were so impressed that they asked him to coach them – temporarily. He stayed there for the rest of his working life, combining soccer-coaching with tuition in the university's machine shop. His team had great success. In thirteen seasons it did not lose a game and it was unbeaten between 1932 and 1941. 'We ain't got a chance against your boys,' Jeffrey was quoted as saying in Brazil, 'but we're gonna fight to keep down any cricket score. We've got to take it on the chin if we are ever going to get anywhere in soccer in the United States. Nobody takes us seriously in this Cup. But we came to Rio to learn.' In Belo Horizonte it was England who would be taught a lesson.

It really did look, before the game, as if everything favoured England. The mountain air was good and clean and instead of having to stay in an ordinary hotel, the whole team were guests at an English-owned gold mine nearby at Morro Velho. What did work against England and their many crack players was the nature of the pitch.

Belo Horizonte now has an enormous stadium which can hold over a hundred thousand people, but in those remote days it was a wretched little ground, cramped and ill-equipped, with a bumpy and uneven field. The dressing rooms were so primitive that the England players preferred to change in a hotel; the Americans, some of whom had stayed up dancing until two that morning, changed at the stadium. One of them asked an English journalist whether he had brought along a cribbage board, to keep the score. At the time his fear that it might be a one-sided game seemed justified.

Only a few weeks before in New York, America had lost 1–0 to a Football Association team whose strength was about that of an England third eleven; its players exhausted by a fourteen-hour journey from Canada. Stanley Matthews was in that F.A. party and only at the last moment was this great player, now thirty-five years old, called to the colours in Brazil. Unfortunately, Mr Arthur Drewry, who was functioning as sole selector of the team, didn't call him up against America.

Drewry has been blamed for his choice of team, but this seems terribly unfair. After all, Matthews apart, it was surely the best team England could have put into the field. A team of reserves, playing for their places, might have put more passion into their game, but what would have been said if the reserves had lost? England, really, could blame no one but themselves and their poor finishing for their eventual humiliation.

England's manager, Walter Winterbottom, would later say, 'Everybody who saw the game would say that England didn't take its chances, dozens of them, and when a team doesn't take its chances, it doesn't deserve to win. Our forwards tried too hard. For the first twenty minutes, they were shooting in, then they began to worry, we must have a goal, they thought. For superiority to show, one must have a good pitch.'

But all this tends to belittle the American achievement. They had a marvellously determined defence, with Borghi a superbly agile goalkeeper and Colombo, playing in black gloves, a strong and determined centre-half. In front of them, John Souza, at inside-left, played throughout with a skill and economy which put the famous England inside-forwards to shame. England, playing in red shirts to avoid a clash of colours, predictably attacked from the first, hit the post and seemed sure of a hatful of goals. But helped by the rough pitch and their own sometimes robust methods, the American defence held out.

Thirty-seven minutes gone and still, astoundingly, no English goal. Then, eight minutes from half-time, the incredible happened: America scored. When Walter Bahr, the American left-half, drove the ball into the English penalty area, there seemed nothing to fear:

Bert Williams, the acrobatic blond keeper, clearly had it well covered. But somehow, suddenly, the ball was deflected by Larry Gaetjen's head, Williams was on the wrong foot, and the ball sneaked into the net.

Was it a fluke? Did the ball just happen to hit Gaetjens on the head and roll in? Some people thought so. But Walter Bahr always insisted that this was exactly the kind of goal which Gaetjens had made his speciality, that it happened far too often to be mere chance. Whatever the truth, the goal stood; and it was the only one of this extraordinary game.

England have always claimed that they equalized and that the goal was denied them. But whether or not they were ill-used, they had to take the blame for keeping the ball far too long in one place and, when a chance did arise, either shooting carelessly or not shooting at all. In the second half switches were made. Roy Bentley, the fair-haired Chelsea centre-forward, who used to drop deep for his club in a way well ahead of his time, was moved out to the right wing. The electric Mortensen was put in at centre-forward and the beautifully balanced and elusive Finney at inside-right. But all this brought was Ramsey's free kick after Mortensen was chopped down in full flight; a clever lob, well headed by Jimmy Mullen, scrambled clear when it had seemed to cross the line. A corner, and no more, was awarded. At the final whistle, the little ground was invaded by hundreds of spectators while newspapers burned on the terraces in celebration of a famous and amazing victory.

'The Americans,' said Stanley Rous, 'were faster, fitter, better fighters.'

'This,' said Bill Jeffrey, with natural but misplaced optimism, 'is all we wanted to do; this is what we need to make the game go in the States.'

But it still hasn't gone.

In its own way, the decisive match of the 1950 World Cup was almost as great a shock as England's defeat by the United States. Indeed, a number of Brazilians died of heart attacks. Defeat for Brazil was unthinkable. All they needed was a draw and a point to top their Final Pool and win the trophy. What could stop them? They were playing wonderful football. They had scored six goals against

Spain and another seven against Sweden. Nothing like it had ever been seen in the history of the World Cup.

The inside-forward trio of Zizinho, Ademir and Jair was matchlessly brilliant; three players whose superb ball-control, pace, mutual understanding and finishing power had routed the Spanish and Swedish defences. HOW TO RESIST? asked the headline in an Italian sports daily, plaintively.

If anybody could resist in the massive new stadium of Maracana, it was the Uruguayans. They knew Brazilian football inside out and earlier that year had fought three close matches with Brazil in the Rio Branco Cup, winning 4–3 in São Paolo and losing by only 3–2 and 1–0 in Rio. The previous year, by contrast, one of their periodic players' strikes forced them to field a team of so-called amateurs in the South American Championship, losing 5–1 to Brazil.

But since then the team had thrown up three remarkable new young players, the little, hunched, moustached right-winger, Alcide 'Chico' Ghiggia, the inside-right, Julio Perez and the tall, thin, pale inside-left, Juan Schiaffino, who had glorious control, passed superbly, and added to these qualities a devastating shot.

Certainly the Brazilian manager, the dedicated and severe Flavio Costa, was taking nothing for granted. 'The Uruguayan team,' he warned, 'has always disturbed the slumbers of Brazilian footballers. I am afraid that my players will take the field on Sunday as though they already had the Championship shield sewn on their jerseys. It is not an exhibition game. It is a match like any other, only harder than the others.'

The Governor of Rio, who gave a public address just before the great game in the Maracana Stadium packed to over-capacity with 200,000 spectators, was by no means as restrained. Indeed, the sheer arrogance of his words shocked Vittorio Pozzo, who had only recently given up his long-held post as *Commissario Tecnico* of the Italian team: now knocked out by Sweden.

'You Brazilians,' cried the Governor, 'whom I consider victors of the tournament, you players, who in less than a few hours will be acclaimed champions by millions of your compatriots ... you, who have no equals in the earthly hemisphere ... you, who are so superior to every other competitor ... you, whom I already salute as conquerors.' The Uruguayans were clearly offended long before the end of this stupid tirade and if it had any effect at all on the Brazilian players, it can only have been to inflate their sense of certainty.

But nothing is certain in football; not even in a World Cup decider played on your own soil in front of 200,000 dancing, chanting, ecstatic fans, beating out their samba rhythms in the expectation – no, the assurance – of victory.

Neither team played the third back game, each had a mobile, attacking centre-half. In defence Brazil played something they called the diagonal system, which, as its name suggests, involved a kind of pivotal play, with the two flank defenders – they'd have been wing-halves, rather than full-backs, in the Brazilian fashion – using a swivelling, zonal, system. In other words, you marked the space rather than the man, which was fine when you were attacking, but rather dangerous when you were not.

Still, why should the Brazilians worry? Up until then Uruguay's form had been pretty indifferent. They had been greatly helped by the fact that their only first round game had been the ridiculously easy 8–0 win over Bolivia, but even so had made very heavy weather of their first two games in the Final Pool, only drawing 2–2 with Spain and being very lucky to win 3–2 against Sweden. Brazil, of course, had thrashed both those teams.

But there was plenty of talent and experience in the Uruguayan team; an acrobatic goalkeeper in Maspoli, a superb flank-defender (left-half in the Uruguayan set-up) in the little black Rodriguez Andrade, nephew of the 1930 star, and a magnificent centre-half in the giant Obdulio Varela, who had been an international for ten years.

Varela, who'd begun his career as an inside-left, was not only physically a very strong player, but was also skilful and deft, a fine captain and a superb example to his team, who would need all his inspiration in a difficult first half.

As expected, Brazil's dazzling, short-passing inside-forward trio set about the opposing defence from the first. They were strongly supported by their fine attacking right-half, Carlos Bauer, and sometimes varied their game with sharply angled twenty-yard passes to the wings.

Varela, wholly defensive at this stage, was solid as a rock, with Andrade, a wonderfully agile and brave assistant. As for Maspoli, he made save after gymnastic save. In the sixteenth minute, a goal seemed imminent when there was a colossal scramble in the Uruguayan penalty box, but Andrade strode into the middle of it and hoofed the ball clear. Seven minutes later, Jair, who rejoiced in beating opponents with an arsenal of tricks, let fly a thundering shot, but Maspoli flung himself across goal and tipped it for a corner. A further wild confusion in the Uruguayan goal-mouth was eventually cleared by Varela.

The next danger came from Brazil's right-winger, Friaca, who took a corner and, when the ball came back to him, shot into a crowded goal area. But again Maspoli saw the ball in time, plunged among the swinging legs and turned it, too, for a corner. True, even he seemed lost when he faced Ademir, deadliest of finishers, alone, yet though the shot was strong and well placed Maspoli got there.

The difficulty with football, however, is that the more you press without getting a goal, the more you lay yourself open to giving one away on the break. So it was that Ghiggia flew away up the right and combined with Miguez, his centre-forward, to make a chance for Juan Schiaffino. A tremendous shot forced Barbosa, the agile Brazilian goalkeeper, to make his first real save of the match. It was a warning.

Then it was all Brazil again and the closest call yet; another corner, a shot by Jair which rebounded from the post. With seven minutes left to half-time, some of the steam seemed to go out of the frustrated Brazilian attack and Uruguay came back into the game. Suddenly Schiaffino was dribbling swiftly and devastatingly through Brazil's far from concrete defence, ending with a fiendish shot which produced another fine save from Barbosa. Half-time, and Uruguay had held out. It was still 0–0.

Only two minutes after half-time, however, their goal finally fell and the floodgates seemed about to open.

Ademir and Zizinho were the architects of the goal. Quickly and cleverly working the ball through on the left, they drew the Uruguayan defence, for once out-flanked when the ball was switched to the right, and there was Friaca running in, full pelt, to shoot, score and send the great stadium into thunderous rapture.

But football is won by the head as much as by the legs and the truth was that, having held out so long and launched such impressive attacks of their own, even if few in number, the Uruguayans lost their sense of inferiority. They clearly believed they could still win. As Rodriguez Andrade, one of their chief heroes and a star of the 1954 World Cup, said afterwards, 'Our team is a strange one. It is capable of anything. Against Brazil, we did not keep back one drop of sweat, but what else could we have done?'

Effort alone, though, is never enough to win football matches at the highest level; Uruguay had a great deal more to offer. Now they went into the attack. The Brazilian defence survived two raids, then a lovely, accurate through pass by Schiaffino sent Perez haring through for a terrific shot which Barbosa just kept out with his finger-tips.

The huge Varela, who had for so long been the bulwark of Uruguay's defence, had begun to move menacingly into attack. The risk could have been costly. Given more space and scope, the Brazilian wingers, Friaca and Chico, frolicked for a while and Andrade made a marvellous recovery to tackle the flying Friaca. But the sight of Ademir, waving his arms frantically at his colleagues, was clear evidence that the tide was turning.

After sixty-five minutes it turned with a vengeance. Varela ran the ball into the Brazilian half, then sent Ghiggia racing down the right wing. Bigode, insufficiently supported, couldn't stop him – the weakness of the diagonal system – Ghiggia crossed to an unmarked Schiaffino: two steps, an irresistible shot and the score was one all.

The life had gone out of Brazil, though; thanks to the faultless refereeing of the Southampton headmaster, George Reader, the game never even began to get out of hand. Now Varela was running the game in midfield, a Titanic figure. With eleven minutes left, Chico Ghiggia gave the ball to Perez, got it back and, running on to it, drove it past Barbosa for the winning goal. Uruguay had won the World Cup for the second time, after a twenty-year interval.

'We knew,' said Varela afterwards, 'that we were technically and individually inferior to the Brazilians. After the victories won by them against Sweden and Spain, we gave up our plans to use a third back method of defence and relied on the old tactics. With a few modifications borrowed from the third back game, we succeeded in erecting a cage, from which the Brazilian forwards were rarely able to escape. How many times did Ademir manage to get away from me? When he did, there was always Andrade or Tejera to cover up. Our plan was to see that every Brazilian forward must beat at least two players before being able to shoot. We accomplished this, thanks to the acceleration, the speed, the timing of Andrade, who seemed to be everywhere, and who brought off some remarkable recoveries. Without him, our countermeasures would inevitably have failed.'

The 1954 Final was just as great a surprise. As we know, Germany had reached the Final despite being thrashed 8–3 by Hungary in the first round and had picked up remarkably well, though Yugoslavia, beaten 2–0 in Geneva, had pressed them hard in the quarter-finals. Then Austria were annihilated 6–1 in the semi-finals and the stage was set for a second match between Germany and Hungary. Games between these two embattled rivals were to become a feature of World Cups.

Few outside the German camp doubted that Hungary would win. They had been hot favourites from the start, the best team Europe had seen since the war, scorers of thirteen goals in two matches against England. They were a veritable attacking machine, which, to the famous skills already associated with Hungarian football, had added that of great finishing power: exemplified by Puskas's devastating left foot, Sandor Kocsis's heading and the shooting of the deep-lying centre-forward Nandor Hidegkuti, who had scored three of the six goals against England at Wembley the previous November.

Add to this a four-in-line defence, an exciting attacking right-half in Bozsik, dazzling wingers in Budai and Czibor and you had a team indeed. Most of it, moreover, played for the Budapest Army club, Honved; taken from their own original clubs to form a nucleus for the international side which was yet another advantage. Of the leading players only Hidegkuti was not a Honved man.

Puskas, however, had not played since being kicked on the ankle in the first German game and although Czibor had moved inside very effectively to take his place, Hungary's passage to the Final had been altogether tougher than Germany's. In the quarter-final they had had to survive what came to be known as The Battle of Berne, when they got into a fearful brawl with the Brazilians and had then gone on to play a glorious but taxing semi-final against Uruguay in Lausanne. A game which both Puskas and Varela missed through injury and one which went thrillingly and tiringly into extra time. So in terms of physical condition at least the Germans, whether they were taking stimulants (as some people believed) or not, would be the fresher.

Then there was the question of Puskas, the Galloping Major, a tubby little fellow who captained and dominated the Hungarian team. Puskas did not yet seem fit, and although the team was playing perfectly well without him, he insisted on playing and did. As substitutes were not to be permitted in the World Cup for another sixteen years, this was a considerable risk.

Moreover, the fact that Puskas and the right-winger Budai were not the greatest of friends meant that Budai, who had been playing very well, was left out of the side. The Germans had no such problems and were a formidably strong team, both in the physical and tactical sense, with the skipper, Fritz Walter, skilfully knitting things together in midfield; with the bull-like Helmut Rahn and the rapid Schaefer incisive and dangerous on the wings; and Morlock and Otmar Walter, Fritz's younger brother, snapping up chances in the middle. Turek had shown himself an excellent goalkeeper, as he would again, and if there was no one in the defence to match such future German stars as Paul Breitner, the attacking full-back, and the remarkable Franz Beckenbauer, at least every member of it was tough, effective and determined. Hungary at their best would beat such a team; but with the doubts about Puskas and the exhausting nature of the quarter- and semi-finals they'd just played, would they be at their best?

At first it looked as if they would. Within eight minutes, they were two goals up in Berne and it began to look as if another eight goals were in prospect. But Germany began well too, three times threatening the Hungarian goal and showing no trace of anxiety. Then Bozsik sent Kocsis clear with one of his intelligent passes. Kocsis's shot hit a defender in the back and the ball fell to Puskas's left foot. The shot was a formality.

Two minutes later, an awful double blunder in the German defence gave Hungary their second goal in circumstances which would have demoralized most teams. Kohlmeyer, the left-back, whose goal-line clearances had saved the Germans against Yugoslavia, mis-hit his back pass and, to make things worse, the ball sprang out of Turek's hands. This time it was Czibor who accepted the gift: 2–0.

Most teams would have lain down and died, but not Germany. Their morale was tremendous. It took them only three minutes to get back a goal – evidence, as in León all those years later, that a German team two goals down is as dangerous as an expiring snake.

Hans Schaefer crossed from the left, Helmut Rahn returned the ball to the middle, Bozsik went for it but could only deflect it into the path of Morlock who stretched out a leg and prodded the ball past Grosics. The game was wide open again.

Hungary, it now grew clear, were by no means at their best. Puskas's ankle was plainly bothering him, he looked ponderous and strangely slow, while Czibor, who had been switched to the right wing, wasn't happy there. Things would improve when he went to his preferred left flank after half-time, but the error of omitting Budai was obvious enough.

Soon after the quarter-hour Germany got their equalizer. Fritz Walter, a superb taker of corner kicks, as the Austrians had found to their cost, took one, another and a consecutive third. Up went his brother, Otmar, but he missed it, as did Gyula Grosics, the Hungarians' daring keeper. Rahn didn't; when the ball reached him, the big outside-right smashed it into the goal.

Now Turek, in the German goal, began to make his great contribution to the game. Kocsis got in one of his typical headers, but Turek bravely reached the ball, then had the luck of the brave when a shot by Hidegkuti struck the post. Now Germany attacked, and for a full three minutes, but Hungary held out and the half-time score remained at 2–2.

Over to Turek again, as the Hungarians began the second half of this exciting, rain-soaked game with a new and furious assault on the German goal. Twice Turek saved brilliantly from Puskas – surely the fully fit Puskas must have scored when he found himself alone in front of goal – and when Toth beat the keeper, there was Kohlmeyer atoning for his previous error by kicking off the line. Turek had another stroke of luck when Kocsis got his golden head – in the figurative sense – to a cross by Toth, but the ball skidded off the bar.

Hungary badly needed to score in that period of pressure. As it was they began to look tired, and the Germans increasingly carried the fight to them. When the Hungarians did strike again it was in a breakaway, a burst by Czibor, his shot blocked by Turek, a loose ball for Hidegkuti; and he missed.

It was crucial. Five minutes later, away down the left raced Hans Schaefer. His high cross flashed over a seething goalmouth seeming to touch Otmar Walter's head. Lantos, the big blond left-back seemed to have the ball, then hadn't. It came to Rahn who coolly controlled it, advanced and, with his less familiar left foot, crashed it past Grosics.

Frantically the Hungarians tried to equalize. Then only two minutes later came the most controversial and, as it turned out, decisive moment of the game. A superlative through pass by Toth took the big German centre-half, Posipal, out of the game and sent Puskas haring through the gap. This time the tubby little inside-left had Turek alone to beat and beat him he did: 3–3, or so it seemed. But the Welsh linesman Mervyn Griffiths' flag was up. As the Hungarians embraced, Bill Long, the tall Cambridgeshire referee, another in the line of Rous and Reader schoolmasters, disallowed the goal. Many thought Puskas well on-side, but there was no appeal and the decision is argued to this day. A last fine burst from Zoltan Czibor, finished with a strong shot, was punched away by a leaping Turek and the Hungarians were beaten. Like Brazil in 1950 and 1982 they had to be content with finishing the 'moral' victors of a superb tournament.

For a surprise to match that of the United States' victory against England, however, you must move on to the 1966 World Cup when North Korea defeated Italy and then, in the quarter-finals, gave Portugal the most colossal fright.

Before the 1966 finals began, few gave a thought to North Korea, which was very foolish. Warning had been duly served in Phnom Penh, Cambodia, where the North Koreans had played Australia to decide which should go through from the vastly depleted Afro-Asian group. Australia are neither African nor Asian, but the quirks of the competition decreed that they should play in that group, from which every other team but they and the Koreans withdrew in protest. They wanted, and eventually got, a separate group for Africa and Asia. By the time it came to the overpopulated 1982 World Cup, each group had not just one qualifier, but two: the price the new FIFA President, the controversial João Havelange, had had to pay for Third World support in his electoral campaign.

So it was decreed that North Korea should play the Australians twice on neutral territory to decide which of them should go to England. Few doubted that the Australians would come through comfortably. They had much more experience and no one had ever heard of the North Koreans, all of them nominally Army officers, kept in closely supervised training in the capital of Pyong Yang.

In the event, the little men of North Korea played dazzling football against an Australian team which looked dull and clumsy by comparison. The Koreans won the first game by a thumping 6–1, the second 3–1; Sir Stanley Rous, the FIFA President, who had watched the matches, told everyone to take them seriously. He was ignored, as was Jean Vincent, outside-left in the splendid French team which took third place in the 1958 World Cup. North Korea, he announced, were a better team than France had been in 1958.

By chance the North Koreans played up in the North East at Middlesbrough, a town well used to good football and great players such as Wilf Mannion and, captain of England, George Hardwick. The local supporters took these mysterious men from Communist Asia to their hearts, referring to them as 'us'.

North Korea did not begin too well. They seemed physically overmatched and slightly bewildered. None of them spoke any English; they parried questions with a smile. All they'd had on the way to England in the nature of warming-up matches was a couple of games in Communist Eastern Europe, but it soon transpired that they'd learned quite a lot nonetheless.

Their first match saw them faced by Soviet Russia, North Korea's patron; the Russians certainly looked much too big for them and beat them 3–0, the big strikers Malafeev and Banichevski scoring all the goals.

Against Chile the Koreans did much better, forcing a draw and almost winning. Then came the third and final game, pitting them against the Italians who'd had a string of impressive victories on their way to the tournament. Just before it started, however, the Italians 'unofficially' sent the drug testing committee a sample to analyse. The doctors in charge told them very forcibly that whatever substance was contained in the sample was certainly illegal. Does this explain the Italians' feeble play? We can never be sure, but tongues wagged.

Edmondo Fabbri, the tiny Italian coach, nicknamed Topolino, the little mouse, had said that the only thing the Koreans had to offer was speed. Yet surprisingly, instead of choosing fast men of his own, he picked two slow and ponderous centre-backs in Janich and Guarneri. He also took the unwise step of choosing Giacomo Bulgarelli, the Bologna inside-forward, who was obviously unfit. Substitutes, you will remember, were still not allowed.

The Italians had been beaten 1–0 by Russia in the previous game and were looking weary, but all they needed to qualify in second place for the quarter-finals was a point and it seemed unthinkable they would not get it.

It soon grew clear, however, that the North Koreans had been learning very fast and were technically a much better team than the Italians anticipated. The Italian midfield of Bulgarelli, Gianni Rivera and Fogli was a clever but fragile one, and they found it hard to dominate and protect their slow defenders.

After little more than half an hour, Bulgarelli ingloriously tried to foul an opponent, but succeeded only in aggravating his injured knee and was carried off. So the Italians were left with ten men against a rapidly improving opposition whose goalkeeper, Myung, had already proved himself in splendid form whenever there was any danger in the penalty area.

Forty-two minutes had gone when Pak Doo Ik, the North Korean inside-left, whose name has been starkly etched into the history of Italian football, tackled Rivera, advanced with the ball and with a powerful cross-shot beat the Italian goalkeeper, Albertosi. The Koreans were delighted; the Middlesbrough crowd overjoyed. What they undoubtedly liked about the Koreans as much as their lively play was their supreme sportsmanship. They never committed nasty, deliberate fouls and when they suffered them at the hands, or boots, of their opponents, they looked surprised and aggrieved, as though they simply hadn't expected such deliberate bad behaviour.

If the Italians were ashamed of themselves – and a volley of tomatoes when they sneaked into Genoa Airport by night showed what their fans thought of them – they found some consolation in what happened in the quarter-final at Everton.

Portugal, the North Koreans' opponents, had played some magnificent football against an ageing, ill-chosen, vulnerable Brazilian team, beating it on the same ground and by the same score 3–1 as it had been beaten by Hungary. Eusebio, the lithe, handsome, superbly fast and graceful inside-right, had already proved himself one of the finest strikers in the tournament, yet within twenty minutes the Koreans, playing wonderfully effective football, had gone into a 3–0 lead and the game looked as good as over.

That first twenty minutes probably showed some of the best and most exhilarating football ever played in a World Cup. The Koreans scored in the very first minute, cutting open the Portuguese defence with a dazzling right-wing move, concluded by a powerful shot from Pak Seung Jin. The success of the goal stemmed from a manoeuvre the Koreans had tried before; very simple, but highly practical. Li Dong Woon, the winger, drove the ball hard into the middle of a packed defence hoping for a useful rebound. This he duly got; Han Bong Zin pushing the ball back from the right to set up the goal. Pak Seung Jin very skilfully made himself room by turning back to the edge of the penalty area, then shot high into the left-hand corner.

Astonishingly, the little men from Pyong Yang should have been two up in five minutes. As the baffled Portuguese struggled to contain their clever attacks, made up of swift, short passing, speed off the mark and fine ball-control, Yang Sung Kook, the left-winger, made himself a splendid chance, then passed instead of shooting.

But the second Korean goal was only delayed. It came when Pak Doo Ik slipped the ball precisely forward to Yang Sung Kook who gave a ground pass to Li Dong Woon and in it went again.

José Torres, the Portuguese centre-forward, was a huge man who lives up to his name – a Tower by name and nature – but the comparatively tiny North Korean defenders, Ha Jung Won and Rim Yung Sum, showed amazing capacity to jump and defeat him.

Taking a short ball from Han Bong Zin, the left-winger Yang Sung Kook glided past two men, held the ball until the last possible moment and then, as a tackle came in, banged it right-footed into the roof of the net.

Only a great player could have turned the tide and, fortunately for Portugal, they had a great player. Eusebio now began to play the North Koreans virtually on his own, moving from the right wing to the left, the left wing to the middle, using his wonderful footwork, swerve and powers of acceleration to get through and round a defence which so far had been equal to everything thrown at it.

After twenty-eight minutes he snapped up a through ball from his gifted little left-winger, Simoes, and made it 3–1. Then, when Torres was chopped to the ground, Eusebio put in the penalty and, in his eagerness to get on with the game, grabbed the ball and ran back to the centre circle with it, to be rebuked on the way, no one knows quite why, by an outraged Korean.

After fifteen minutes of the second half, Eusebio broke through to score again. Next, he was brought down and scored another goal from the penalty spot. The Koreans, too generous and naive to mass in defence and defend their big lead, were paying the price.

Now Eusebio was rampant. His penalty had come after an electrifying left-wing run in which he skipped past tackle after tackle, so superbly that to foul him seemed the only way of stopping him. Then came a fifth goal, to rub salt in the Korean wounds, scored after a corner by José Augusto, the right-winger turned inside-forward. So the North Koreans went out gloriously, leaving vibrant memories.

Yet for those who have always upheld the right of the 'little' countries of Afro-Asia to take part in the World Cup finals, hoping to encourage their native game, the sequel was disappointing. The North Koreans retired to Pyong Yang and haven't been seen in the World Cup finals since. Instead of building on their marvellous performances against Italy and Portugal, they sank back into isolation, as often as not offering strange political reasons for not taking part in tournaments; distressingly, when they did next play, they were no more than the modest little team they'd been expected to be in England. The memory of their brave brilliance in 1966, however, remains.

So does that of Algeria's gallant 2–1 victory over West Germany in Gijón, in the first round programme of the Spanish World Cup of 1982. Unfortunately, in the modern World Cup a result like that, for all its glory, can lead to absolutely nothing at all. The Algerians hadn't been expected to get anywhere. Indeed, at a Press Conference only the day before the match, Jupp Derwall, the German manager, laughed out loud at the mere thought of their even forcing a draw, but they won fair and square. They were, indeed, fair to a degree. They didn't need to be anything else, for in no way were they technically inferior. They played good, counter-attacking football, subdued the much-praised German strikers, Littbarski, Hrubesch, the subtle Rummenigge and incisive Fischer and had in the elegant Lakdar Belloumi the best player on the field.

Belloumi had not come to the World Cup unknown. A skilled inside-forward, excellent on the ball and clever in distribution, he had been voted African footballer of the year in 1982 – a great distinction in a continent which, despite its disappointing lack of good teams, has produced many marvellous individual players.

'At the beginning,' said Herman Neuberger, West Germany's FIFA delegate, after the game, 'you don't want to believe such a thing, then I was staggered and, at the end, my stomach started hurting.'

The Algerians began cautiously, clearly aware that they were facing a powerful and illustrious team, holders of the European Nations Cup and co-favourites with Brazil for the World Cup itself. Algeria marked man to man, seldom stirring from their own half until they realized there clearly wasn't much to fear. As one Spanish reporter remarked, the West Germans were a machine, some of whose parts were not working.

Gradually and unobtrusively, Belloumi began to take over the game. Stationing himself in the midfield, he sent clever, angled passes to his two excellent wingers, Madjer on the right and Assad on the left, each a sore trial to the German full-backs who were always happier (especially Manny Kaltz) going forward in attack. But that is one of the odd features of modern football. Full-backs are expected to overlap to make up for the general lack of wingers; when they do meet a true winger, with pace and skill, they are often baffled.

Rummenigge moved increasingly into the middle beside the massive Hrubesch, but the Algerian stoppers were no more intimidated by him than the tiny North Koreans had been by Torres, all those years ago. Long, high crosses into the middle are, in any case, usually a sign of defeat and the Algerians had little trouble dealing with them. At half-time there were still no goals, which was in itself a heartening achievement for Algeria.

The second half saw the German defenders and midfielders still bombarding the Algerian area with high balls intended for the starkly visible blond head of Hrubesch. But these opened up the possibility of counter-attack. Zidane broke away and found Belloumi on the left. Well served by the Courtrai (France) player, Belloumi showed he could shoot as well as scheme, by letting fly a drive which Harald Schumacher, the big German keeper, blocked, but couldn't hold. The ball ran loose to give Madjer an easy goal. Yet again the unthinkable seemed to be happening.

For a quarter of an hour the Algerians held their lead and three minutes later it looked as though Zidane might double it; but he shot into the side netting. German boots were flying, especially Briegel's, a sure sign of growing panic, when suddenly Magath, the inside-left whose goal would decide the 1983 European Cup Final for Hamburg, capped a German breakaway by pulling the ball back across goal. In dashed Rummenigge to equalize and German supporters began to breathe again.

Not for long. The very next minute Algeria roared away for a wonderful winning goal. Assad made a classic winger's sprint down the left, leaving the heavy Kaltz nowhere. The cross was perfect, as was Belloumi's tremendous, instant shot, which left Harald Schumacher standing.

The green and white Algerian flags waved in joy and triumph. Then Merzekane, the Algerian right-back, made a bold attempt to do a Kaltz, thundering through alone, but Schumacher beat him to the ball – just.

Desperate for an equalizer, the Germans now began pressing the well-organized Algerian defence. With a minute left, a shot by Rummenigge smacked against the bar; then the mighty blond Briegel came pounding through from defence for a tremendous shot. It was saved by Cerbah, the Algerian goalkeeper. There was to be no last-minute reprieve for the Germans. They had been well and truly beaten and Belloumi and his two wingers were the stars of an extraordinary game.

The following day a perceptive Spanish reporter praised the Algerians, but noted that they would no doubt pay for their success. So they did, losing their next game to Austria, though they did go on to beat the Chileans later. Alas, they would be excluded from the next round by the disgraceful 'deal' between the Germans and Austrians, playing out that fiasco of a 1–0 win for West Germany which put both of them in the next round, at Algeria's expense.

But the Algerians went out with honour; you could scarcely say as much of the Austrians and West Germans who played such a devious trick on them.

5 Pelé and Other Scorers

There has never been a player like Pelé and probably never will be again. He played in four World Cups, winning three of them, and could have played in five: the Brazilians found it hard to forgive him for refusing to take part in 1974. He made his debut in Sweden in 1958 as a 17-year-old of extraordinary prowess, scored the goal that beat Wales in the quarter-final, three goals against France in the semi-final and a further marvellous two goals against Sweden in the Final. Almost from the first he was an utterly complete player; a supreme technician, superb goal scorer, great shot, acrobat and header of the ball, sharply aware of what was going on around him.

In the 1970 World Cup Final against Italy, he headed the first goal with a leap which would have been the envy of any Olympic high-jumper and created the second and third goals with balls beautifully laid off to Jairzinho and his captain, Carlos Alberto, respectively. He was a player of astonishing originality and in that same 1970 World Cup in Guadalajara came up with two pieces of sheer inventive cheek which no other footballer in the world could have thought of, let alone executed. If one were to classify him, it would be as a second striker, an attacking inside-forward. Despite his fabulous power in the air he was never a centre-forward, and despite his skill on the ball and his immensely quick football brain, he was never an inside-forward in the accepted, midfield, scheming sense. He stayed too far up front and scored too many goals.

He was no saint. He would always have preferred to play pure football, not least because, in terms of pure football, nobody could match him. But if kicked or fouled, he had learned to kick back. It was his declared policy to give as good as he got. Thus in a bruising 1964 'Little World Cup' match in São Paolo against

Argentina, he was so savagely provoked by the fouling of Mesiano, his marker, that he eventually butted him in the face and broke his nose. Afterwards, however, showing that such things did not come naturally to him, he was so overtaken by remorse that he hardly touched the ball for the rest of the game, which Argentina won 3–0.

Injury put him out of all but a couple of games in the 1962 World Cup in Chile and in 1966 he was literally kicked out of the competition by the ruthless Bulgarians and Portuguese. Later when he saw the film of the tournament and realized how appallingly badly and deliberately he'd been fouled in the Portuguese game at Everton he swore he would never take part in another World Cup. Luckily he was persuaded, before 1970, to change his mind.

The son of a not too successful footballer, Pelé was born in the village of Tres Coraçoes in the heart of the huge Brazilian state of Minas Gerais. He soon showed extraordinary skill in the dusty, shanty-town street-games and was taken under the wing of the old Brazilian international forward, de Brito, who'd played for Brazil in the 1934 World Cup. Pelé made progress under him, but didn't really like him because he was what Pelé called 'a shouter'.

A shy teenager, he moved to the club and city of Santos, where he would spend his entire Brazilian career, scoring over a thousand goals. At sixteen he was already a Brazilian international and he was still only seventeen when they took him to the World Cup in Sweden in 1958.

There, injury forced him to miss the opening two games in Pool IV in which Brazil beat the Austrians but an England side well organized by its coach, Bill Nicholson of Spurs, held Brazil to a 0–0 draw in Gothenburg. It was on the same ground that Pelé made his World Cup debut and a splendid one it was.

He did not score against Russia, but with his precociously cool head and amazing technique and opportunism he instantly made a notable difference to the game. Early on he shot against the right-hand post and later he exchanged passes with Vavà, sending that forceful centre-forward through to score the second goal in a 2–0 success. Then, in the quarter-final again in Gothenburg, he got the curiously flukey goal which eventually beat a brave

Welsh team, defending valiantly and obliged to play without their formidable centre-forward, John Charles, who was injured. Pelé's shot would probably have gone wide had it not hit the boot of Stuart Williams, the Welsh right-back, and been deflected past their fine goalkeeper, Jack Kelsey.

But it was against France in the Stockholm semi-final that Pelé and Brazil really came to life. True, Brazil were helped by an injury to the polished French centre-half, Bob Jonquet, who had to leave the field after thirty-seven minutes, when the score was 1–1, and Raymond Kopa, the gifted little French centre-forward, was causing Brazil's uncertain central defence immense problems; but Brazil deserved to win nevertheless.

In the second minute of the game, Didì, Garrincha and Pelé made Vavà's devastating goal, but Fontaine had equalized within nine minutes. For the next twenty-eight minutes the score held level. Then Jonquet went off (no substitutes in those days, of course) and almost immediately Brazil recaptured the lead. Didì scored again within a couple of minutes and Pelé then weighed in with a devastating hat-trick.

To score three goals in a World Cup semi-final at the age of seventeen, even against a depleted opposition, is a stupendous achievement. But Pelé did still better in the Final against Sweden. He refused to be intimidated by defenders such as the blond left-half Parling, the 'Iron Stove', whose gruesome foul in the semi-final had sent the unfortunate German captain, Fritz Walter, to bed. Even when, in the second half, he found himself in the thick of a crowded penalty area he showed no fear at all, just caught the ball calmly on his thigh, hooked it over his head and before it had a chance to touch the ground, crashed it past the helpless Swedish goalkeeper, Svensson.

The fifth and last Brazilian goal in this majestic display was Pelé's too. Zagalo, who would be his manager in 1970, crossed from the left wing and up went Pelé, magnificent and irresistible, high, high above the Swedish defence, to head the ball home. As he'd also had a shot against the post, he might well have had a hat-trick in this game as well.

His achievement left him the most famous player in the world – at the age of seventeen. He remained almost touchingly modest and naive, but unfortunately people took advantage of him. He made large sums of money, but twice was financially tricked and ruined. On the second occasion in 1975, he was obliged to come back to football with the New York Cosmos. The contract was worth millions of dollars, but the poor fellow was millions of dollars in debt. He has stayed in the States ever since and even presented the American case for hosting the World Cup to FIFA, in Stockholm in May 1983, fruitlessly as it turned out.

After all that had gone before, the 1962 tournament was a terrible anticlimax. Brazil played in the newly built jewel of a stadium in Viña del Mar, where samba bands beat out their monotonous rhythm through every game, where pelicans sat on the rocks and the sea mist drifted in across the ground. Brazil were now an older and more cautious team, the tireless Zagalo playing so deep on the left that it was virtually a 4-3-3 rather than a 4-2-4 formation. Pelé made a masterly beginning in the opening game against Mexico, who nonetheless gave Brazil a good deal more trouble than had been expected.

Reversing the play of the 1958 Final, Pelé crossed and Zagalo, untypically, headed in for the first goal. Pelé himself scored the second, a prodigious shot, beating four defenders before crashing the ball past Carbajal, the veteran Mexican keeper.

Then came the game against Czechoslovakia: and disaster. After twenty-five minutes, Pelé took a pass from Garrincha and, twenty-five yards out, sent a tremendous shot against the foot of the post. Then he limped off the field and out of the 1962 World Cup.

He was replaced by the twenty-four-year-old Amarildo who did wonderfully well. True, there was no substitute for Pelé, there never has been, but Amarildo scored vital goals, not least the narrow-angled equalizer against the Czechs in the World Cup Final. In the second half of this Final Amarildo was again the decisive figure. Boxed in on the left-hand goal-line, he beat his man with a sudden turn from left to right, centred across the exposed goal with his right foot, and there to head into the empty net was the attacking right-half, Zito. Brazil took the lead.

'*Con Pelé o sin Pelé tomaremos Nescafé*,' was the slogan painted on the Santiago buses when Chile were due to play Brazil in the semi-finals: 'With or without Pelé we shall drink Nescafé.' As it transpired, Brazil won without him.

In 1966, they were again soon reduced to playing without him and didn't even reach the quarter-finals. English referees gave Pelé no protection at all. In the opening game against Bulgaria at Everton, Pelé scored a spectacular goal from a typical free-kick in the first half, Garrincha adding another in the second. Besides the enormous power of his right foot, Pelé had the ability to bend or swerve a dead ball, in the best Brazilian manner. But his fitness had been in doubt before the competition and the harsh attentions of Zhechev, his Bulgarian bodyguard, did him no good. 'Pelé,' said a French journalist with prophetic gloom, 'won't finish this World Cup. It's amazing he hasn't gone mad.'

He was injured badly enough to miss the next game, in which an inspired Hungarian team, with Florian Albert, a terrifically versatile centre-forward, and Farkas, who scored the most superbly hit goal of the World Cup, beat the Brazilian holders 3–1 – their first defeat since 1954. Pelé returned in the third game, against Portugal, but a disgraceful double foul by the Portuguese defender, Morais, put him out of the running. The indulgent English referee, George McCabe, gave him no protection at all and even allowed Morais to stay on the field. So Pelé accomplished little and Portugal won 3–1. To be fair, despite the loss of two superb defenders, Portugal had a strong team: fine players such as Augusto, Simoes, Torres, Coluna, their splendid captain, and Eusebio, Europe's rival to Pelé in spectacle and efficiency; and the match had been lost and won long before Morais's brutal and totally unnecessary double foul. An ill-chosen, ill-advised Brazilian team, managed by the 1958 coach, Vicente Feola, were well and truly out of the Cup.

Mexico in 1970, however, saw Pelé back on his most glorious form. Having won his battle with the original manager João Saldanha, who had bitterly criticized him in public, contemplated dropping him altogether and then been replaced himself in favour of Pelé's old team mate, Zagalo. From then on Pelé got on swimmingly. His form in the group games in Guadalajara was quite staggering.

In the opening game against Czechoslovakia (the team Brazil

had beaten in the 1962 Final) Pelé almost scored one of his most daringly impertinent goals. Noticing that Viktor, the generally effective Czech goalkeeper, had a habit of coming far off his line when the play was upfield, Pelé, with an amazing fifty-yard lob, sent the ball over Viktor's head, to bounce just wide of the goal post.

Shortly after half-time Pelé did score; though not as sensational as a goal from the lob would have been, it was still spectacular. Gerson, with his superb left foot, sent a long ball into the Czech penalty area straight to Pelé who caught it faultlessly on his chest, spun and volleyed it into the net. Only two such masters of the game can make goals look so easy.

Pelé was obviously in wonderful form, which he demonstrated again when Brazil met the World Cup holders, England, in Guadalajara in the cruel heat of noon. Outrageously, FIFA had given way to the demands of European television and decreed that games be played at this ridiculous hour. It was particularly difficult for teams from Northern Europe. Used to playing at sea-level they already faced the problem of altitude (the thin air tends to make you gasp for breath); now FIFA's ludicrous and potentially dangerous decision condemned them further to melt in the torrid heat.

Pelé, though admirably well marked by the Londoner, Alan Mullery, whom he would congratulate after the game, was unstoppable. It was certainly no fault of Mullery's that Pelé was responsible for the only goal of the game. Tostão probably handed off Bobby Moore, England's splendid left-half and captain, but the referee gave no foul and Tostão, concluding a run which took him past three English defenders, drove the ball into the goalmouth. There, Pelé deftly laid it on for Jairzinho, who came roaring in from the right to score.

More memorable still, however, was Pelé's first-half header, and Gordon Banks's save. Jairzinho, the powerful Brazilian outside-right, left Terry Cooper standing, dashed on to the goal-line and crossed. Pelé headed the ball on the bounce just inside the left-hand post and was already shouting, 'Goal!' when Banks, with incredible, gymnastic agility, somehow got across his goal from the opposite post and tipped the ball over the bar.

Better supported in attack and midfield than he had been in Sweden twelve years earlier, Pelé continued to torment defenders. He didn't actually score in the quarter-finals against Peru, though Brazil's third goal came just after half-time, when his long shot was deflected home by Tostão.

In the semi-finals against Uruguay, held again to the Uruguayans' understandable fury in Guadalajara, which was by now a home from home for Brazil, Pelé almost brought off another incredible goal. Racing through on the admired Uruguayan keeper, Mazurkiewicz, he daringly sold him a dummy; with fiendish inventiveness he ran away from the ball to one side of Mazurkiewicz to confuse him, while allowing the ball to run on the other. The keeper was confused all right: he was drawn away from the ball, as Pelé intended, but when Pelé caught up with it, he shot fractionally wide.

Earlier in the game, having shrewdly and typically noticed that Mazurkiewicz tended to kick the ball out short to one of his defenders, Pelé lurked with intent, intercepted one of these clearances and volleyed splendidly, only for Mazurkiewicz to make an astonishing save.

It was a bruising game in which the Brazilians came in for a lot of rough treatment. The first half left the teams level at 1–1; in the second half, however, Jairzinho gave them the lead and Pelé cleverly made a third goal, drawing the defence before rolling the ball to Roberto Rivelino, who scored without trouble.

In the Final against Italy, Pelé climbed early to Rivelino's cross to head a phenomenal goal. The Italians, hardly in the game, snapped up Clodoado's careless backheel to equalize just before half-time. But after Gerson put Brazil ahead again it was one-way traffic, and Pelé set up two dramatic goals for Jairzinho and Carlos Alberto. He had had a wonderful World Cup, better even than his hat-trick debut of 1958, and good enough to make up for the disappointment of having had to miss games in both 1962 and 1966. You could hardly blame him for not wanting to play in 1974.

Pelé may have been one of the stars of the 1958 World Cup Final, but the leading scorer of the competition, setting a record which has not been beaten yet and probably never will be, was France's Just Fontaine, with thirteen goals. Four of them, it is true, were scored in Gothenburg against West Germany in a third place match which the Germans took far less seriously than the French, but thirteen goals are still a formidable achievement, as were the nine he had scored before the third place match.

Fontaine went to Sweden with the French team, quite reconciled to being no more than a reserve. France hadn't won a game all year and when they arrived at their training camp at Kopparberg, where their 1930s World Cup star Alex Thépot was a selector, Fontaine wryly remarked, 'I'm only centre-forward till Kopa comes.'

Until his release by Real Madrid, Kopa had reluctantly been playing on the right wing, but it was as a deep-lying forward rather than an out and out striker that he wanted to operate. So when René Bliard, another candidate for centre-forward, kicked the ground in training, hurt his ankle and went home singing Fontaine's praises, Fontaine got his chance. The door was suddenly open for a superb partnership. Dark, squat, with a fine turn of pace and a devastating left foot, Fontaine proved the ideal foil for Kopa, cleverly anticipating and exploiting his superb passes.

The opening game against Paraguay at Norrkoping, the town which had produced Liedholm and the Nordahl brothers, showed the strength of the French team. Paraguay actually scored first and were level 2–2 at half-time. Thereafter the deadly combination of Kopa and Fontaine, well supported by Roger Piantoni at inside-left, reduced them to pulp. Another five goals and Paraguay were annihilated in a crushing 7–3 defeat. Three of the goals went to Fontaine who, timing his runs to the split second, placed his left-footed shots to perfection.

In the next game, at Vasteras, France surprisingly lost 3–2 to the Yugoslavs, but you could scarcely blame the high-scoring Fontaine, who added another two goals to his tally. Next came a hard game against Scotland. Bill Brown, coming into the Scottish goal, won both Kopa's and Fontaine's admiration, while Tommy Docherty, playing wing-half in his second World Cup, said that the French inside-forwards were 'like greased lightning'.

By way of returning past favours, Fontaine made the first goal for Kopa with a cross which the little man volleyed in. But Scotland struck back forcefully. John Hewie, their South African born defender, hit the post from a penalty kick and it was well for France that in the very last seconds of the first half Fontaine got away for another of his cool, characteristic goals. On this occasion, however, it was not Kopa who put him through, but Bob Jonquet, the centre-half. The second half produced just one goal, scored for Scotland by Baird, and France were in the quarter-finals.

There, they came up against a weary Northern Ireland. Several of their best men had been injured, they badly lacked a decent centre-forward and their plight was made worse by the absurd decision to send the team a crazy 210 miles to Norrkoping by coach. Ireland, too, unlike the French, had had to play off against the Czechs to reach these quarter-finals, and all in all they were no match for the lively French.

Just once, early in the game, the Irish almost got the goal they so badly needed to inspire them to rise above their exhaustion. In one of their well-planned set-piece throw-ins, Danny Blanchflower threw the ball to Billy Bingham's head (one future Irish team manager serving another), Bingham flicked it on to Jimmy McIlroy who had a chance to score, but squared it instead of shooting.

That was that. A splendidly compact, fast, clever French team took over, scoring four times. Three of those goals came in the second half and two of them were snapped up by Fontaine.

So to the terribly difficult semi-final in Stockholm, against Brazil. Fontaine got yet another goal, equalizing Vavà's, after eleven minutes, but, as we know, Jonquet limped off after thirty-seven minutes and that was that.

There was only the third place match to come, and in this, Kopa and Fontaine sliced the German defence open at will, a fair indication (despite the fact that Germany were below full strength) of what might have happened had the teams been drawn against one another in the semi-final.

In my mind's eye I can still see Fontaine being sent through the wilting German defence time after time by Kopa's beautiful passes and almost always making full use of them. Four times he scored; France ran off winners 6–3, and Fontaine had his honoured place in the history of the World Cup. His partnership with Kopa had been one of the most formidable the competition had ever seen.

If Fontaine's record has stood since 1958, Geoff Hurst's has stood since 1966 and seems no more likely to be beaten: three goals in a World Cup Final. The West Germans still insist that it was only two, that Hurst's second goal, the first scored in extra time, bringing the score to 3–2 and virtually giving the World Cup to England, was not a goal at all.

Like Fontaine in 1958, Hurst started the 1966 World Cup finals with no great hope of playing. Indeed, unlike Fontaine, he did not even figure in the first three games.

Hurst was born in the North of England in Ashton-under-Lyne, son of an Oldham Athletic half-back. His family moved to Essex when he was still a child and thus the tall and very muscular young boy was trained at West Ham United as a wing-half. Though well coached in the West Ham style under its manager Ron Greenwood, Hurst was not an outstanding wing-half and at one point West Ham almost sold him to a Second Division team. Greenwood countermanded the decision. When Hurst was switched to inside-forward or second striker, lining up beside the centre-forward, Greenwood was proved right.

Suddenly Hurst started to score and make openings for other players. He was a magnificent shot with either foot, had sufficient pace, the ability to climb huge heights like the classic English centre-forward and a lively footballing intelligence which enabled him to move skilfully into space, often on the left, and open up the game for his colleagues. Yet he was only a marginal choice for the 1966 World Cup squad and had a poor, clumsy game against Denmark in Copenhagen, in the pre-World Cup tour of Europe.

His real chance came in the quarter-final against Argentina at Wembley after Jimmy Greaves, never Alf Ramsey's favourite player, had been hurt in the previous game against France. Hurst took that chance superbly. It was his first competitive match since Copenhagen and he found it hard to fit into the team's rhythm at first, particularly as the Argentines were playing a deliberately spoiling, callous game, breaking up England's flow with a myriad of petty fouls. Moreover, he was getting very little decent service from midfield. Even when Rattin, the Argentine skipper and attacking centre-half, was sent off for badgering the referee, England still could not break down Argentina's tough defence.

Four minutes after half-time, however, Ray Wilson, England's lively, attacking left-back, took a pass from Bobby Moore, Hurst's West Ham team-mate, and dropped a long, high centre over the defence. It landed at Hurst's feet and at first seemed almost to surprise him. But he recovered in time to drive a terrific shot just inside the right-hand post, only for Antonio Roma to spring across his goal and make an exceptional save. It was the first really dangerous English shot of the match.

It began to look as if England would never beat Argentina's ten men, but with thirteen minutes left, Wilson gave the ball to Hurst's other West Ham colleague, Martin Peters, who'd also been a late addition to the team. Peters, a technically faultless player, curled in a glorious high cross and this time, at the near post, Hurst responded with a gigantic leap, a fine, glancing header, which landed in the opposite corner of the goal and put England into the semi-final against Portugal.

Whilst the semi-final between West Germany and Russia was a wretched parody of football, the match between England and Portugal, if it fell short of the glories of Hungary and Brazil, was a tribute to the game. The England team, at last moving smoothly and vigorously, was worth far more than the 2–1 win it achieved. Eusebio, the tournament's leading scorer, was simply blotted from sight by the tenacious Stiles, while Bobby Charlton, who scored both England goals, had his best game of the World Cup, perhaps even the best he ever played for England. The second goal, coming only eleven minutes before the end, was superbly created by Hurst. Forcefully shaking off Carlos's challenge, he went to the right-hand goal-line, pulled the ball back and Bobby Charlton's right foot struck a fulminating goal. England were through to the Final.

Hurst didn't know till the Friday whether or not he would be playing in it. Greaves was fit again, and Roger Hunt, the Liverpool inside-forward, determined, dedicated and very dear to Ramsey, had played in every game. At last, on the Bank of England ground at Roehampton, Ramsey announced his team. It was unchanged. Hurst would play.

And how he played! Germany went into the lead when Helmut Haller scored after Ray Wilson headed a cross straight to his feet. But it was Hurst who equalized.

Moore, always so alert, curled a swiftly taken free-kick into the German penalty box and before the defence had woken up, Hurst, equally sharp and timing his run to perfection, dashed in from the right and turned the ball past Tilkowski in goal, with his head. Three minutes before half-time, Hurst's strength in the air almost gave England the lead. He jumped above the German defence and flicked the ball to Hunt on the far post, but it came to Hunt's weaker left foot – the shot hit Tilkowski's hopeful, upraised arms and bounced away.

You simply could not keep Hurst and his dynamic finishing out of this game. Twelve and a half minutes before the end of normal time, Alan Ball, who was playing with equal dynamism, bundled the erring German goalkeeper, Tilkowski, over the line to get a corner, which he took himself, from the left. Out of the scramble, the ball ran loose to Hurst whose shot was instant, strong and accurate. Weber, the German stopper, lunged for it and the ball curled into the air, almost as if it were on a jet of water. Peters got to it first and scored: 2–1.

The match seemed over, but in its very last seconds Herr Dienst, the Swiss referee, gave a rather doubtful free-kick against England's tall, fair, centre-half Jackie Charlton, Bobby's older brother. There was just as good reason to think that Held had backed into Jackie Charlton as vice versa. Be that as it may, there was a fearful confusion round the English goal, after Emmerich's free-kick, a strong left-footed shot, hit Schnellinger in the back and finally ran loose for Weber to equalize.

Exhausted, as much by the drama and tension of it all as by the running, the England team lolled on the thick Wembley turf, waiting for extra time. Alf Ramsey pointed to the Germans, who seemed in a worse plight still. 'Look at them!' he said. 'They're finished!'

Whatever the truth of that, England found new life and dash in extra time. After a hundred minutes a fine long pass, by Nobby Stiles of all people, went to Alan Ball on the right wing. Ball would later write that at that moment he thought, 'Oh, no, I can't get that one! I'm finished!' but somehow he found the strength and sped past Schnellinger to cross on the turn.

As usual Geoff Hurst was in the right place. As the ball

reached him on the near post, he met it with a furious, instant right-footed shot. Tilkowski hadn't a hope of reaching it. The ball tore past him, hit the underside of the bar and came down ... Where? In front of or behind the line? Roger Hunt had no doubts. He immediately raised his arms in celebration in the goal-mouth, making no attempt to follow up.

Herr Dienst was not so sure. Besieged by violently protesting West German players, he went to his linesman, the silver-headed Bakhramov, a splendid, distinguished figure; with immense emphasis Bakhramov pointed his flag towards the centre. A goal it was, a goal it remained, but the Germans haven't accepted it to this day.

Hurst, however, was to get another. In the final moments of the game with the Germans pressing frantically for the equalizer, hurling all their troops into battle and leaving great gaps in their defence in consequence, a long, shrewd pass by Bobby Moore sent Hurst galloping through again, this time right down the middle. Spectators were running on to the pitch behind him to celebrate, a clear breach of regulations. Hurst didn't see them. He dashed on alone, finally letting fly a fearsome left-footed shot which tore high past Tilkowski, making it 4–2 and giving Hurst his record. He was the first person to score three goals in a World Cup Final, and the Cup itself had at last come to the country where football began.

As we have seen, England's two goals in the preceding semi-final were scored by Bobby Charlton, another record maker, who would play in three World Cups and become England's leading, aggregate scorer of all time.

Certainly he was one of the great heroes of 1966. He had been switched from outside-left where his natural gifts of pace, body swerve, fine footwork and magnificent shooting from either foot, had made him formidable. Ramsey had turned him into England's midfield player, the nerve centre of the team. He wasn't a great creative inside-forward in the traditional sense. Johnny Haynes, who'd been his captain and inside-left in Chile in 1962 and had also played disappointingly in Sweden in 1958, was much more that type of player – a hitter of superb through and crossfield balls. Though he would sometimes excite the crowd with mighty, crossfield balls, swept across Wembley's wide expanses to the opposite wing, Charlton's passing was never very imaginative.

What he did so well was to beat opponents with his skill, speed and agility, taking out one defender, drawing another and creating the conditions for a dangerous attack. Alternatively, he could break through from deeper positions to score spectacular goals. He was in fact a natural left-footer, who had trained his right foot to be just as devastatingly powerful and precise. It was in fact with his right foot that he answered the chants of the Wembley crowd in England's second game against Mexico in 1966 as they cried: 'We want goals!'

Charlton responded with a searing, right-footed cross shot from well outside the area, which flew high and wide of the keeper, into the far corner of the Mexican goal. England had broken their duck after 128 minutes' play; in their opening game, they had drawn a dreary 0–0 with Uruguay.

Charlton should actually have played in four World Cups. His exclusion from the 1958 tournament was ludicrous. True, he'd suffered an appalling shock earlier that year, in February, when he had been one of the few survivors of the fearful Munich air crash. The Elizabethan aircraft carrying the Manchester United team back from a European Cup fixture in Belgrade, taking off from Munich in bad, snowy conditions, failed to gain sufficient height and crashed into a hut at the end of the runway, killing and injuring many of its passengers.

Thus, at a cruel stroke, England were deprived of eight of their team including their captain and left-back, Roger Byrne, Tommy Taylor, their goal-scoring centre-forward and the magnificent Duncan Edwards, a huge, driving left-half who was still only twenty-one and was expected to be one of the stars of the World Cup. Among others who died was the excellent little right-half, Eddie Colman, who could well have figured in England's World Cup party, while, as we have already seen, Northern Ireland were robbed of Jackie Blanchflower.

For the shy, sensitive, 20-year-old Charlton, the crash was a horrifying blow. Indeed, it took him years to recover. At the World Cup tournament in Gothenburg, which began only months after the crash, he still seemed in a state of shock. England had picked him for a pre-World-Cup match in Belgrade where, in baking heat, they were annihilated 5–0, and Charlton was among several who did not distinguish themselves. That might have been a good reason for not putting him, then a striking inside-left, in the initial line-up, but it was no reason at all for keeping him, and his scoring power, on the sideline for the whole tournament.

So he had to wait till 1962 and Chile, to play his first World Cup game, in the seedy little town of Rancagua, as an outside-left. By the second game, against Argentina, Charlton was in dashing form. After seventeen minutes, he crossed from the left, Alan Peacock, the tall, new centre-forward, headed neatly on and when Navarro, the stopper, handled, Ron Flowers scored from the spot.

It was with a brisk, low, right-footed shot that Charlton, cutting in from the left, scored England's second goal before half-time. They finished 3–1 winners, qualifying for the first time since 1954 for the quarter-finals, when Brazil beat them 3–1 in Viña del Mar.

Four years later, in the semi-final at Wembley, Charlton scored both England's goals against Portugal. It was his best and most versatile performance of the World Cup and showed him at his most dangerous. As always, his shooting was superb, but on this occasion his passing almost matched it and he ran beautifully with his splendid, easy, graceful action.

After half an hour, a shrewd pass by the left-back, Ray Wilson, sent Roger Hunt clear. Pereira could only block the shot and Charlton coolly drove the ball back into the goal. Portugal had a lively, dangerous spell after half-time, but the England defence held out strongly, the initiative was regained and eleven minutes before the end, Bobby Charlton scored again – an instant, right-footed shot.

In the final stages, Portugal pressed, England wilted, but Charlton, in a breakaway, almost scored again: this time with a left-footed drive which Pereira stopped but couldn't keep, the ball running loose, but not to an Englishman. A penalty by Eusebio when Jackie Charlton handled was all the consolation Portugal could gain.

In the 1970 World Cup, in Mexico, Hurst played his heart out, though Charlton, in fine, incisive form, was foolishly pulled off the field by Ramsey in the last quarter-final against West Germany.

Hurst showed his opportunism had not left him when, in the opening game against Rumania, in Guadalajara, he refused to be intimidated by a harsh, bruising Rumanian defence, smartly and strongly winning the match with a left-footed shot in the second half, his fifth World Cup goal. Charlton had a very good game, his best in midfield for England for a long time; only the previous year, by contrast, when the team toured South America, he'd seemed to be running out of steam.

In the next game, lost 1–0 to Brazil, Hurst uncharacteristically threw away a very good chance. Clean through the Brazilian defence, he made the elementary mistake of presuming he was offside, hesitating, then, eventually, shooting hastily and weakly. The heat that day was appalling. At León in the quarter-final, the combination of heat and altitude made conditions even worse.

England's 4-4-2 methods, which relied heavily on overlapping by the full-backs, were of doubtful value in such exhausting conditions; and the West Germans, after an early stutter against Morocco, had been playing exceedingly well.

But England began well, getting a goal which was marvellously set up and scored by their right-half, Alan Mullery, after half an hour, and adding a second five minutes after the break when Geoff Hurst, in excellent, unselfish form, sent Newton, the right-back, racing down the wing, as he had in the first goal. This time Martin Peters slammed in the cross.

Now the game changed, becoming less easy for England. Hurst had been too fast, mobile and strong for Fichtel, his marker, in the first half so Helmut Schoen, Germany's manager, taking shrewd advantage of the new availability of substitutes, brought the tough Willi Schultz on to mark him instead.

When Beckenbauer shot under Peter Bonetti's body to make it 2–1, Ramsey unwisely pulled off Charlton, evidently to keep him fresh for the anticipated semi-final; it is true that he was showing slight signs of weariness. But now, especially with Grabowski coming on at outside-right, the pendulum swung sharply in West Germany's favour.

Hurst, who thrived on centres to the near post, had had far too few of them, but with the score still at 2–1, Colin Bell, Charlton's substitute, provided one. Hurst stooped to it at the right-hand upright and his header flashed past the German goalkeeper, Sepp Maier; and just wide of the other post. Germany, however, won in extra time thanks to Gerd Muller's volleyed goal, to make the final score 3–2.

I shall not easily forget the taxi drive back to Guadalajara, with Geoff Hurst: how drained, dehydrated and exhausted the poor fellow was. If anybody ever gave his all in a game, it was surely Hurst in León. Moreover, when, in extra time, Francis Lee beat Schnellinger on the right-hand goal-line and pulled the ball back for Hurst to crash it home, there had seemed no clear reason why his goal should have been disallowed. He could not possibly have been offside.

In Germany's next game, the semi-final against Italy in Mexico City, goals would fall like leaves in extra time and Germany, with Beckenbauer crippled, would go down 4–3. Even Muller and his opportunism could not save them: while England, it transpired, had played in their last World Cup finals for twelve long years.

6 Goalkeepers

A wise German once remarked that in a football team there were ten men and a goalkeeper. Goalkeepers, in other words, are different. It has even been said that goalkeepers are crazy!

Their contribution to the tournament has been enormous, their impact on the game considerable, and no history of the World Cup would be complete without goalkeepers' stories; their marvellous saves and amazing mistakes, the goals they have stopped and those they have conceded. Amongst the most remarkable goalkeepers were Ricardo Zamora of Spain who, as a veteran in the 1934 World Cup, showed that he was still among the greatest and bravest keepers in the game; Dino Zoff of Italy, who played in the 1982 World Cup at the age of forty; Gordon Banks of England, whose save from Pelé in Mexico was one of the best ever seen in a World Cup; Lev Yachine, the massive, black-jerseyed Russian, who played in three World Cups, making some marvellous saves and some peculiar mistakes; Antonio Carbajal of Mexico, who played in no fewer than five tournaments, and Felix of Brazil, who looked uneasy and unhappy throughout the World Cup finals of 1970, yet came away with a gold medal.

One famous goalkeeper actually lost his chance to play in the 1930 World Cup which his team won. Masali had kept goal superbly in the 1928 Olympiads and was one of the principal reasons why Uruguay, fielding their full international team in Amsterdam, kept their title. For two whole months before the 1930 World Cup these so-called amateurs stayed in a hotel in the middle of the splendid Prado Park with its 150,000 trees, just outside Montevideo.

The curfew was strict, even married men were not allowed to spend the night with their families. Masali got bored. One night he slipped into town, came back later and, shoes in hand, was tiptoeing through the hotel back to his room, when suddenly he came face to face with the team's trainer. He was thrown out of the hotel and the squad immediately, despite the fact he was much the best keeper in Uruguay. His place, and a gold medal, went to the reserve keeper, Enrique Ballesteros.

There were many good goalkeepers in the 1930 tournament. One of them was the brave and graceful Frenchman, Alex Thépot, who would play again in France's solitary first round match against Austria in 1934.

France opened the competition on 13 July with a game against Mexico. France won 4–1, but for Thépot it was a disastrous game. After only ten minutes a Mexican forward kicked him on the jaw and he was forced to leave the field. He suffered severe concussion for a whole day, but the following day was back in goal for the bruising match against Argentina. For twenty minutes the hardy Thépot performed miracles, saving shot after shot as the Argentine team, hot favourites to win, bombarded the French goal.

France resisted the siege far longer than expected, eventually going down just when they were looking good, to a very unlucky goal only nine minutes before the end. Argentina were given a free-kick and when Monti placed the ball and shot, the French were taken unawares, forgetting the recent decision that a referee need not whistle for a kick to be taken. Moreover, Marcel Pinel, the French centre-half, who had played wonderfully well against the thuggish Monti, took a step to his right, unsighting Thépot, and the ball flew past him into the net. Thépot kept reminding Pinel of his mistake for the next thirty years!

Ricardo Zamora, alas, did not play in the 1930 World Cup, for Spain refused to participate. Even at this early date, he had been a major star for ten years, having played superbly in the 1920 Olympic tournament in Antwerp. He also took part in the Olympiads of 1924 and 1928, but his solitary match for Spain on British soil in 1931 was a disaster.

Two years earlier, in the fierce heat of Madrid, Spain had become the first foreign team ever to beat England, winning 4–3, with Zamora in goal. In all he played forty-seven games for Spain, thirty-one of them consecutively, giving away only twenty-seven goals in his first thirty-four matches. He was small for a goalkeeper, but his agility, courage and positional skill made up for that.

In the Highbury mud, however, he made a couple of dreadful early mistakes, conceding two soft goals and eventually another five – England romped home 7–1. Dixie Dean, the England centre-forward, magnificent with his head, recalled later that at the reception that evening Zamora had told him through an interpreter that he was 'nothing in Madrid tonight', to which Dean rather unkindly replied, 'Tell him he's not much here either.'

Against Italy, in Florence, in the 1934 World Cup quarter-final, Zamora was at his best. He played a wonderfully brave, resourceful game, despite being given very rough treatment by the Italian forwards and little protection by the referee.

Before the game, his name had buzzed on the lips of thousands of Italian fans in cafés and bars throughout the country. Was he, at thirty-three, the same, elastic Zamora? Would he frustrate Italy again, as he'd done so often in the past? Certainly the Press found him to be more mellow. Ten years earlier, when asked who would win the competition at the Olympics in Paris, a Basque beret on his head, he'd replied, 'We shall win, of course!' Now, ten years later, he replied to the same question, 'I've no idea. Who can tell?'

Once, in the twelfth minute of the game in Florence, he was beaten, but Quincoces, a full-back almost as famous as Zamora, was there to kick off the line. Then it was Spain who took the lead with a weird goal. Langara, the Spanish centre-forward, took a free-kick, Regueiro, the inside-left, lunged at the ball, miskicked it, and managed to beat the distinguished veteran Italian goalkeeper, Giampiero Combi, who had prepared himself for the obvious, straightforward, shot.

By half-time, Italy had forced sixteen corners to a mere couple by Spain, but time after time Zamora came off his line, to pluck those corners out of the air. A minute after half-time he was beaten. Pizziolo, the Italian right-half, sent the ball high into the goalmouth. It seemed to present no danger to Zamora, but as he went for it, he was plainly obstructed by the Italian centre-forward, Schiavio. His weakened clearance went straight to Gioanin Ferrari, who drove the ball home.

The game went into extra time, when the Italian play became

almost violent. The score was still 1–1 at the end of the 120 minutes, but Zamora was so ill-used he could not take part in the replay – staged the very next day. Noguet, Zamora's knee-padded substitute, played a fine game, but could do nothing about the only goal, finely headed by Meazza from a corner by Raimondo Orsi.

Czechoslovakia, who reached the Final in 1934 where they gave the Italians such a very hard run, had another of Europe's leading goalkeepers in the smallish, sturdy Frantisek Planicka, another player whose lack of height made no difference to his acrobatic excellence. But just as Combi was caught out in Florence in 1934 when Regueiro miskicked the shot, so poor Planicka was undone in the Final by the incredible shot with which Orsi scored the equalizer.

It took two glorious saves by Planicka to get the Czechs through in their first-round game against Rumania in Trieste; in those days it was a knock-out tournament. The Rumanians surprised everybody with their quick, inventive play, took the lead in eleven minutes and were unlucky to go down 2–1 in the end, not least because the second goal came when Sobotka, the Czech centre-forward, won the ball in a bounce-up by the referee.

The Czechs knew they would have to do better and in Turin, against Switzerland, they played what was regarded as the best match of the second round. Planicka's goal was bombarded after the clever Czechs had established a 2–1 lead, till eventually Trello Abegglen, the lively inside-left, beat him. The Czechs took over the game again and Nejedly, once described by a French journalist as an inside-left 'as pure as Bohemian crystal', scored the winner.

Next Planicka faced the strong, methodical, but somewhat unimaginative Germans in the semi-final. It was not one of his finest games. Nejedly gave the Czechs the lead, but after eighteen minutes of the second half, when they seemed well in control of the game, Noack, the German inside-left, took a long shot which Planicka, for some strange reason, simply stood and watched as it sailed over his head: 1–1. The Czechs, however, recovered, won 3–1 and reached the Final.

At the Rome Final they frightened Italy exceedingly. Playing in the classical, so-called Danubian, short passing style, with Cambal attacking strongly and cleverly from centre-half, they were slightly the better team in the first half. There was no goal, however, until twenty minutes from the end of normal time when Puc, the left-winger, took a corner and, after the ball finally came back to him out of the crowded goalmouth, drove it home to give the Czechs the lead.

How close they came to winning! Sobotka had a fine chance to beat Combi, but missed; Svoboda smacked a shot against an Italian post. Italy were wilting, but with only eight minutes to play, the left-winger Raimondo Orsi, an Argentine international, scored his freakish goal.

Taking a pass from Guaita, another Argentine, who played at outside-right, Orsi, slim and rapid, went through the Czech defence, feinted a shot with his left foot, but shot with his right. Somehow he brought off an astonishing swerve which quite foxed Planicka. The goalkeeper leaped desperately for the ball, touched it with his fingers, only for it to swirl over them and into the net, while behind the goal Vittorio Pozzo danced his delight.

Seven minutes into extra time, Schiavio, though exhausted, found sufficient strength to bang in a centre by Guaita and the unlucky Czechs had lost. Outside Italy, the Italian victory was none too popular. 'Over the whole championship,' wrote the Belgian referee, John Langenus, 'there brooded a certain spirit: Italy wanted to win – it was natural – but they allowed it to be seen too clearly.'

By 1938, Italy had an excellent new goalkeeper in Aldo Olivieri, while the gallant Planicka was still playing for Czechoslovakia.

One of the most interesting and unusual goalkeepers of the 1938 tournament was the Cuban, Carvajales. This was the only World Cup the Cubans had yet qualified for and it was known that Carvajales was a man to admire. He was said to combine the calm, sure gifts of Rudi Hiden, the great Austrian keeper (who oddly enough had been ignored by Austria in 1934), with the courage and acrobatics of Zamora; such, at least, was the view of reporters who watched him play for Cuba in Toulouse against Rumania. Carvajales was in exceptional form and though the score at full-time was 1–1 the final result was an exciting 3–3 draw.

Cuba's first equalizer came only five minutes before the end, but in extra time both teams scored two goals, Rumania happy to get the final equalizer. Despite the golden reports and his great reputation, the Cubans dropped Carvajales from the replay.

Benito Carvajales didn't seem at all put out. The night before the match he called his own private Press Conference, at which he said, 'We shall win the replay, that's certain. The Rumanian game has no more secrets for us. We shall score twice, they will only score once. *Adios, caballeros!*'

Surprisingly enough, he was right. The Rumanians were ahead at half-time, but in the second half Cuba did score twice though the French linesman Georges Capdeville, who would eventually referee the Final, was sure the winning goal was offside.

Carvajales returned for the second round game against Sweden, at Antibes, and must have regretted it. The Swedes thrashed the Cuban team 8–0. Gustave Wetterstroem, 'the Bombardier of Norkopping' and forerunner of the great Gunnar Nordahl, his blond hair flying, shot furiously and justified his nickname with four dramatic goals.

At 5–0, the French journalist, Emmanuel Gambardella, later President of the French League and a man who'd been to Uruguay in 1930, solemnly closed his typewriter. 'Up to five goals,' he said, 'is journalism. After that, it becomes statistics!'

Cuba missed a penalty, Carvajales hadn't a chance with any of the goals and the Cubans sailed for home. On the way they stopped in New York to watch Joe Louis sensationally revenge himself on Germany's Max Schmeling and win the world heavyweight title.

Oddly enough, when the 1938 tournament began, Vittorio Pozzo was said to have lost confidence in the Italian goalkeeper, Aldo Olivieri. But in the difficult opening game against Norway, in Marseilles, Olivieri's goalkeeping was one of the chief reasons Italy survived. Vittorio Pozzo has told how in the very last minute of normal time, with the scores level, Brunyldsen, the massive Norwegian centre-forward, found himself with Olivieri alone to beat and let fly a tremendous high shot to the right of the goalkeeper. Olivieri responded with a magnificent leap and save which Pozzo described as 'one of the finest and certainly, as far as results were concerned, the most "important" of the whole tournament'.

Spectacular goalkeepers loom large in the history of Italian football, amongst them Dino Zoff, who played for Italy in three World

Cups – the third in Spain at the age of forty – and who was admired above all for his calm professionalism.

A quiet, decent, self-contained man from the North East of Italy – like Enzo Bearzot, his team manager in two World Cups – Zoff could be as acrobatic as anybody when the occasion required, but by and large he preferred to make things look as easy as possible. It is argued that by the time of the 1978 World Cup, in Argentina, he was not at his best – he seemed then to be vulnerable to long shots. In Italy's decisive second-stage game against Holland, at the River Plate Stadium in Buenos Aires, he was beaten by a drive from the edge of the box by Erny Brandts, the young Dutch centre-back, who scored an own goal in the first half. Later he was beaten again from still longer range by a tremendous right-footer from Aarie Haan. Italy lost 2–1.

In the third place match against Brazil, Zoff was again beaten by two shots from far out. One, an amazing, swerving drive from a difficult angle on the right by the right-back, Nelinho, which swirled past him in a crazy parabola; the other, a left-footed swerver from outside the penalty area, by Dirceu. Yet Zoff had had his fine moments in the competition too, and by 1982 there was still nobody to rival him. 'Zoff,' said one Italian critic, 'has suffocated a whole generation of goalkeepers.'

There were times in the 1982 World Cup Final against West Germany when he was very uneasy on crosses, yet in the dramatic match against Brazil in Barcelona, when his skills were truly needed, he showed he was still the most formidable of goalkeepers.

Sadly, no Brazilian came to shake Zoff's hand after the game, not even the brilliant midfielder Falcão, who'd been playing in Italy for Roma. Indeed Falcão was so bitterly upset by Brazil's defeat he very nearly gave up football altogether and had to be persuaded to go on playing by his mother. This was in sharp contrast with the Italy game against Norway, held in Marseilles all those years ago in 1938. Then, according to Pozzo, when Brunyldsen had got over his initial surprise and disappointment at Olivieri's glorious save, he went up to him and proudly shook his hand in recognition of a great footballer. (In a similarly sporting gesture the Portuguese shook Bobby Charlton's hand after his second goal in the 1966 semi-final.)

When Zoff came to the 1974 World Cup finals in West Germany, he had been unbeaten in international football for just under 1,100 minutes. This amazing record was surprisingly punctured by the Haitian centre-forward, Sanon, in its 1,147th minute. Though Italy recovered to win the game, there was tumult in the camp and after a draw with Argentina, they lost 2–1 in Stuttgart to the admirable Poles and were eliminated.

The Polish goalkeeper was the massive Jan Tomaszewski, who had become a famous figure at Wembley the previous year when his extraordinary goalkeeping, sometimes brilliant, sometimes wildly erratic, kept England at bay, gave Poland a 1–1 draw and took them to the finals. Brian Clough, the outspoken Nottingham Forest manager, commentating on the match, called Tomaszewski 'a clown', and indeed there were times when he and his goal seemed to be saved only by the luck that is said to favour the brave.

There was certainly no question of his courage and in West Germany, he looked very good indeed. He gave a wonderful display against West Germany on a drenched pitch in Frankfurt, when the Germans, undoubtedly helped by the conditions, squeaked through to the Final by a single goal. Tomaszewski, who had saved a penalty by Tapper of Sweden in the previous game, though probably moving before the kick was taken, now saved another one, from Uli Hoeness. But when Hoeness's shot was deflected to Gerd Muller, 'the Bomber', he hadn't a chance. In went the ball for the only goal of a game which, given the wet conditions, should really never have been played.

Unfortunately for Poland, Sepp Maier, the West German keeper, was in just as fine form as Tomaszewski. Maier's World Cup career was a curious one. Had he been fit he would probably have played in the Final against England at Wembley in 1966, for the West Germans were unhappy with Tilkowski. Four years later, however, they were unhappy with the way the blond Maier, with his huge goalkeeping gauntlets, played in their lost semi-final against Italy and he was dropped from the third place game in which they beat Uruguay.

By 1974, however, he was in commanding form and played every game. His double save against the two fine Polish wingers, Lato and Gadocha, in the first half, probably decided the game and put

West Germany in the Final. Here, too, he made a vital save, when he thwarted Johnny Rep, put clean through by Cruyff, not long before half-time.

Maier played his third World Cup in Argentina, but West Germany had a disappointing time. Franz Beckenbauer, their masterly captain and attacking sweeper, had joined the New York Cosmos, who would not release him to play. Maier, like Zoff before him, let in a thirty-five-yard shot by Haan when West Germany drew 2–2 in a fine game with Holland, in the second stage. Who knows how long he might have lasted – as long as Zoff, perhaps – had not a bad motor accident cut short his career.

The true goalkeeping hero of the 1978 World Cup, however, was Argentina's Ubaldo Fillol who, after a shaky beginning, played a wonderful game against Holland in the Final. Indeed, it was the combination of his saves and the superb bursts of Mario Kempes, the attacking inside-left, which won Argentina the World Cup. Late in the first half, Kempes, the only foreign-based player in the Argentine side, a tall, well-built, rangy figure, snapped up a pass from the left by Luque, the big centre-forward, roared through Haan's desperate tackle and scored. Then, just on half-time, the powerful midfielder Johan Neeskens found Rob Rensenbrink in space, Rensenbrink shot hard, but Fillol hurled himself at the ball, reached it and enabled Argentina to take their one goal lead into the dressing room.

Almost immediately after half-time, Neeskens had a tremendous shot from just outside the penalty box, but Fillol reached that too. He couldn't stop the tall substitute Nanninga heading a late equalizer, but in extra time Kempes produced two more goals.

In the first period, another of his inspired runs brought a goal, though Jongbloed, the veteran Dutch keeper, almost managed to seize the ball. In the second period, Kempes's speed and control scattered the Dutch defence again and this time he gave an easy goal to Bertoni.

Jan Jongbloed too was an interesting figure, another of those World Cup stars who initially thought they were just going along for the ride. Indeed, when he was picked for the 1974 tournament, the blond Van Beveren having refused to take part, Jongbloed took his fishing rods with him, assuming he would never get a game.

Indeed, most people thought the chief reason Rinus Michels had picked him was that his good humour kept everybody happy. In the event, injuries saw to it that he played every game and he played impressively. His style was daring and eccentric but in his very daring, his dashes out of his area when the offside trap broke down, he prevented goals that others might have given away. So it was that Jongbloed, the forgotten goalkeeper, the tobacconist, found himself playing in two successive World Cup Finals.

So did Gilmar of Brazil, with the difference that he was on the winning side both times in 1958 and 1962. He was less happy in 1966. Well past his peak, his reflexes much slower, he found himself doing his best to stop the holes in a leaking Brazilian defence and was dropped from the third and final game.

Since then, Brazil have found it astonishingly hard to replace him. Leao, the big fair-haired keeper who played in 1974 and 1978, probably came closest, but Felix, as we have seen, was a very fragile keeper in 1970, making mistakes in Mexico which gave some goals away, while in the opening game against Russia in Spain, Waldir Peres let a shot from the Russian Bal bobble through his arms.

Why is it that Brazil, whose football feeds on the spectacular, should find it so hard to produce goalkeepers? It has been suggested that one reason could be the desire of young Brazilians to score goals rather than stop them; to be another Pelé, rather than a new Gilmar.

Perhaps we never realized the supreme value of Gilmar until, ten long years after he made his debut for Brazil in the South American Championship of 1953, he played behind a rather flimsy defence on tour in Europe and made save after save, not least at Wembley, against England. It was at Wembley, too, that he had saved an England penalty in 1956.

Playing most of his career for Corinthians of São Paolo, he took on a new lease of life when they discarded him and Santos, Pelé's club, picked him up for a song. Gilmar had two things in common with Italy's Dino Zoff: he usually wore a grey jersey and he was a goalkeeper who tended to make things look easier than they were.

Lev Yachine of Russia, a marvellous keeper and a great sportsman, like Gilmar figured in the 1958, 1962 and 1966 World Cups.

I still treasure the memory of him in the semi-final against West Germany in his last World Cup at Everton, standing up, the ball in his grasp, wagging a reproachful finger at a German forward who had come in dangerously close for the ball.

Born in Moscow in 1929, the towering Yachine spent his whole career with Moscow Dynamo, though after leaving school at the age of fourteen he worked in an aircraft factory and played ice hockey. When he was twenty-three years old he saw the Bulgarian goalkeeper Sokolov on tour in Russia. Sokolov was a player who liked to dash out of his penalty area as a kind of unofficial sweeper and boot the ball away when the defence had been beaten by a through pass. Sokolov thus provided Yachine with the inspiration for his own game.

Russia's initial refusal to take part in the World Cup meant that he was twenty-nine before he took part in it for the first time in Sweden, but the impression he made was immediate. How hard it seemed to beat him. Whether on the ground, where his long arms seemed to stretch out forever, or in the air, where he made use of his majestic height. All the more credit to the much abused England centre-forward, Derek Kevan, for soaring above that height and those upstretched arms, to head England back into the game in Gothenburg, from Billy Wright's high free-kick.

That made it 2–1 to Russia. Tom Finney later got the equalizer from the penalty spot. In the eventual play-off, however, held on the same ground, Yachine and Russia had the last laugh. Peter Brabrook, the young Chelsea outside-right, who was playing his first game for England, hit the post twice but both times the ball rebounded. Ivanov, the Russian winger, hit it once and the ball went into the net.

His chance had come from a careless throw by the English goalkeeper, the largely forgotten Colin McDonald of Burnley, who in fact had an excellent World Cup and did not deserve so cruel a stroke of fortune. But this, as Yachine was to discover both in Arica (Chile) and Liverpool, is the fate of goalkeepers. They, of all players on the field, are scarcely ever pardoned for their errors.

In 1962, Russia reached the World Cup quarter-finals, in which they were drawn against Chile, the hosts, then only a moderate team, but passionately supported by their fans. The game was to be played right up in the north of this thin, 3,000-mile-long country, at Arica, almost on the Peruvian border. The Russian morale was not very high. They were a very tightly disciplined, rather lonely bunch, but they seemed likely to beat Chile quite comfortably.

It had already become clear that Lev Yachine was not at his best, not by a long way. In their second game, in what a French sports paper described as 'one of the greatest surprises of modern football', little Colombia had wiped out a 3–0 lead to hold Russia to a 4–4 draw. Early in the second half it was a clear 4–1 to Russia, but after sixty-eight minutes, the impossible happened. Lev Yachine, the mighty Lev Yachine, gave away a goal direct from a corner. The Colombians took heart and, inspired by a marvellous little inside-forward called Klinger, laid siege to the Russian defence. Thus, despite a couple of exceptional saves by Yachine, they drew 4–4. *L'Équipe*, the French newspaper, solemnly said, in their annual publication, that this match 'certainly marked an historic date, the end of the greatest modern goalkeeper, if not of all time: Lev Yachine'.

Just how silly it is to make that kind of blanket statement was shown a little over a year later at Wembley when Yachine, clad this time in a yellow jersey, played the England forwards almost on his own for a full forty-five minutes as the Rest of the World goalkeeper. At half-time, he was replaced; but he had done more than enough to show that he was anything but finished. Three years later he would be back again in England for the 1966 World Cup.

Meanwhile in Arica, he was to make two more appalling mistakes, and this time they would cost Russia the game.

Chile did not play particularly well in front of a fanatical crowd of 17,000, but Russia played worse and Yachine gave away both Chilean goals. Each came from a long shot. After ten minutes, Leonel Sanchez, the left-winger, let fly a powerful left-footed cross shot from a free-kick. It beat Yachine. Chislenko, the Russian winger, equalized from still further out, a good thirty-five yards, but two minutes later Eladio Rojas, Chile's attacking left-half, again from very long range, beat Yachine for the winner.

Though Yachine had certainly had a couple of very uncharacteristic lapses in the game against Chile in Arica, he was, I thought, very unlucky to be blamed by his manager, Morozow, for Germany's second goal in the semi-final at Everton in 1966. In my view, this rotten game was only distinguished by Yachine's fine goalkeeping, which kept Russia in the game, and by his equally fine sportsmanship.

The Russians played most of the game with ten men, and much of it with nine. Sabo, the inside-left, hurt himself early on, when attempting a foul; Chislenko, who had been crippled in a tackle by Schnellinger (which ironically led directly to Germany's first goal), was sent off the field for taking a kick at Siggi Held, who'd hurt him in a fair tackle. The Germans' second goal came when Franz Beckenbauer, their then twenty-one-year-old right-half, curled a beautiful long left-footer round the outside of the Russian wall and in between Yachine and the far post.

England's winning World Cup goalkeeper in 1966 and their World Cup keeper again in 1970 was Gordon Banks. He had two magnificent tournaments, made the save of his life in Guadalajara against Pelé and would almost certainly have prevented England being beaten by West Germany in the 1970 quarter-final at León, had he not drunk that fatal bottle of beer and missed the match, poisoned.

Banks was a quiet, shy Sheffield man who, like so many goal-keepers, had made his name with the little Derbyshire club, Chesterfield. He succeeded the robust and fearless Ron Springett, the 1962 World Cup goalkeeper, whose poor eyesight had made him vulnerable to long-range shots.

Banks, too, was vulnerable to long-range shots at his debut in 1963 against Brazil, at Wembley. Alf Ramsey, his manager, had warned him that the Brazilians struck and swerved their free-kicks, but he was still beaten by a free-kick from some thirty-five yards out from the formidable left foot of the Brazilian winger, Pepe. There were indeed moments like this when Banks would falter; another came in Belgrade in 1965, in a friendly match against Yugoslavia when, at another free-kick, Banks infuriated Ramsey by standing behind his own defensive wall, instead of in the gap it left!

The day before the 1966 World Cup Final Banks announced

at Roehampton that Ramsey had convinced him – 'My mind's not got to wander,' he said. Nor did it. He was a large, bold, tremendously athletic keeper, with no obvious faults, good at going for the high centres as well as plunging about on the goal-line.

It is hard to remember him making a mistake at all in the 1966 World Cup. He played very well when England were under pressure from Portugal in the semi-final, especially when, with Portugal threatening an equalizer, he jumped to turn a right-footed shot by Coluna, Portugal's excellent half-back and captain, over the bar. In the Final against West Germany, his best moment came in the first half when a corner by Siggi Held was poorly cleared. Wolfgang Overath pounced on the weak header and shot, Banks threw himself to block the ball and when Lothar Emmerich, the big left-winger, shot, Banks dived again and saved.

It was against Pelé and Brazil, however, that he made the save of his life. This was his one-handed save in the 1970 World Cup in Guadalajara, now one of the most famous in the story of the game, when somehow he hurled himself across the goal to tip Pelé's bouncing header right-handed over the bar. 'He got up like a salmon out of clear water!' said Banks admiringly, afterwards.

Had he and not Peter Bonetti, who had had weeks without a competitive game and was clearly out of practice, been able to play in León, the results might have been very different.

Twelve years later, when England at last reached the World Cup finals again, England's excellent goalkeeper was the hefty, dedicated Peter Shilton, who had once been Banks's understudy and pupil at Leicester City.

It was a goalkeeper, alas, who provided one of the most displeasing and dangerous moments of the 1982 World Cup. Early in the second half of the semi-final against France in Seville, Harald Schumacher, the West German, came thundering out of his goal as Battiston, the French substitute, a defender, broke on to a through pass and advanced full pelt, alone. Schumacher instantly smashed Battiston to the ground with a wicked blow of the forearm and there the poor fellow lay senseless, the foolish security provisions of the Seville police preventing the Red Cross men from getting to him for several minutes. He might have died, but fortunately did not, though he did lose a couple of teeth and obviously had to leave the field.

Throughout this time, Schumacher totally ignored Battiston, made not the slightest attempt to help him or to find out how he was. Yet both Schumacher and his team got off scot free. Charles Corver, the Dutch referee, had not seen what had happened and his linesman, who surely must have done, did nothing. Otherwise, the French would have had a penalty and Schumacher would have been sent off the field, thus effectively putting France into the World Cup Final.

The Scots, who had been let down by Alan Rough's goalkeeping when they lost to Peru at Cordoba in the 1978 tournament, found him fallible once again in Spain where, after beating the feeble New Zealanders 5–2, they were thrashed by a brilliant Brazil and held to a draw by the Russians, who eliminated them.

That goalkeepers can make or break World Cup teams has been shown, sadly, by the experience of Scotland's teams.

Scotland have done wonderfully well in terms of reaching the World Cup Finals – 1974, when they were knocked out without losing a game in Germany, 1978, when they had a wonderful win against Holland, and 1982. They could have gone to Brazil in 1950. In 1954 they and their goalkeeper Martin let through seven goals against Uruguay in Switzerland, but in 1958 they found in Bill Brown probably the best World Cup keeper they have ever had.

But why this country, which virtually invented the game and had so many grand goalkeepers in the past, has so signally failed to find them in recent years, who knows? Certainly it has cost them dear in World Cup tournaments, when they have so often flattered to deceive, as if the act of qualifying had used up all their physical and mental energies.

7 Brawls and Battles

Given the great pressures of the World Cup, the increasing money and prestige at stake and the constant clash of footballing countries whose idea of the game is so vastly different, it is perhaps surprising that there have not been more violent games in the history of the tournament. Particularly since the good, sound and firm refereeing needed to keep the violence in check has been lacking in recent years. Much refereeing, alas, especially in Argentina and Spain, has been weak and inefficient.

The 1978 Final between Argentina and Holland bordered on lawlessness and the Brazilian, Coelho, in 1982 made as poor a job of refereeing as Italy's Gonella in the 1978 games, even though in Madrid, unlike Buenos Aires, he did not have to contend with the passionate bias of a home crowd.

The organizers of the 1930 World Cup, in Uruguay, were fully aware of the importance of getting referees to use the same criteria as each other in their decision-making. (The FIFA Referees' Committee in 1978 and 1982, by bleak contrast, had a policy of letting supposedly experienced referees decide as they thought best.) So in 1930, on the eve of the tournament in Montevideo, all the referees were brought together for a final conference. Unfortunately, it had little effect, for despite hearty agreement on the importance of uniformity, they all continued to employ any variety of different methods.

Thus, a Bolivian referee, called Ulysses Saucedo, gave no fewer than five penalties in the Argentina v. Mexico game, of which two were perhaps justified. The Argentines won 6–3.

Then, when Argentina played their decisive First Pool game against France, the French left-winger, Marcel Langiller, was in full flight for the Argentine goal, for what could have been the equalizer, when suddenly the Brazilian referee, Almeida Rego, blew the whistle for full-time – six full minutes early! There was instant chaos and, when Rego confessed his error, mounted police had to get the crowd off the pitch before the game could restart. Afterwards, José Andrade, Uruguay's fine half-back (who called Langiller 'a truly great dribbler') said 'The French were the victims of bad luck – and a referee who didn't know much about football. They deserved to win.' Thépot and young Marcel Pinel were carried from the field shoulder-high by admiring Uruguayan spectators, who clearly felt the same way.

When Argentina played Chile in their third game, the fur truly began to fly. Luisito Monti, Argentina's ruthless centre-half, was the initial culprit. He took a kick at Casimiro Torres, Chile's left-half, as he jumped to head the ball, and Torres retaliated. A fierce free-for-all followed, players battling with each other, with even the goalkeepers becoming involved, until large numbers of police rushed on to the field and broke it up.

A number of players were badly cut and bruised but the referee sent no one off and, almost unbelievably, the game was resumed as if nothing had happened. The Argentines conceded a goal through a mistake by their keeper, Bossio. When the final whistle blew, the Chileans advanced and politely shook hands with the winners. It was as if the violence had been purged by the brawl.

The game between Rumania and Peru in Pool III was worse still. Rumania's team had been personally selected by King Carol and, when a number of the players were refused time off to go to Uruguay by the oil companies which employed them, he himself intervened to get them released.

This time it was a Chilean referee called Warken who, right from the start, had little or no control over the game. Every now and then he would award a free-kick, often unjustified, because he seemed to think he should do so at regular intervals.

Mario De las Casas, the Peruvian captain, found this not at all to his liking. His tackling became increasingly violent, his gestures wilder, until Warken finally sent him off after a scuffle in which the Rumanian right-back's leg was broken. This was an error, since De las Casas was not the offender and remained on the pitch for a full five minutes arguing the toss with his trainer. Rumania won in the end 3–1.

The game which everybody feared would turn into a battle was the Final between the bitter rivals from opposite sides of the River Plate, Uruguay and Argentine. 'Victory or death!' the Argentines had chanted in Buenos Aires, as boat after boat left the quayside for Montevideo. 'Not a single Argentine revolver in Uruguay!' was the order to the Montevideo police, who searched supporters both when they arrived and at the entrance to the Centenary Stadium. Indeed, tension was so high that the Argentine players had been under a twenty-four hour guard by the police, ever since the inflamed Argentina v. Chile match.

John Langenus, the respected Belgian referee, an eccentric figure, who usually wore a cap and leggings, had demanded guarantees of safety for himself and his linesmen. In the event, he probably provided the best guarantee of safety himself, for his calm, effective refereeing did more to keep tempers down than all the rifles and bayonets around the Stadium.

The possible flashpoint came, as we have seen, when Guillermo Stabile shot Argentina into the lead with a goal which the Uruguayans and their fans considered offside. Fortunately, however, far from provoking a riot, this seemed to stun the crowd into silence. By the time the Uruguayans ran out the winners at 4–2, it was clear that Langenus had things well in hand and that, blessedly, there would be no trouble, either on or off the field.

In 1934, the Italians were probably the toughest and most provocative team in the competition. Certainly they were indulged by referees, above all in the disgraceful first quarter-final game in Florence, against Spain.

In the same round, in Bologna, Hungary confronted Austria: a meeting of the two traditional foes. 'It was a brawl,' said Hugo Meisl, the Austrian chief, afterwards, 'not an exhibition of football.' Foul succeeded foul. Horwath, a lively little forward, who had been brought in for the game, raced in to give Austria the lead in the seventh minute. Six minutes after half-time, Zischek, 'the Ghost', a clever outside-right, moved into the middle to make it 2–0.

Tension grew. Moments later, Bican of Austria and Toldi of Hungary confronted one another; then it was Horwath and the Hungarian left-back, Sternberg. Dr Sarosi, the well-educated Hungarian centre-forward, then scored from a penalty, making the game tauter still. A foul by Markos, the Hungarian right-winger, got him sent off the field, but the ten Hungarians fought like lions and went down only 2–1 against the calmer Austrians.

Notorious in 1938 was the Battle of Bordeaux between the Brazilians and the Czechs. It was a torrid day. Three players were sent off: Machados and Zeze of Brazil and Riha of Czechoslovakia. Planicka, the famous Czech goalkeeper, broke an arm, while Nejedly, the inside-left, had his leg broken. The Czech right-half, Kostalek, received a nasty stomach injury and two Brazilians, Peracio and the Black Diamond, Leonidas, hobbled off the field at the end.

No one quite knows why Zeze kicked Nejedly so violently and brutally soon after the start. He was instantly sent off the field. Brazil still went ahead on the half-hour through Leonidas but, with a minute to half-time, Riha and Machados were sent off for exchanging blows.

Fifteen minutes after the interval, Domingas Da Guia, the Brazilian full-back, handled and Nejedly scored from the penalty spot, much to the fury of the new Brazilian keeper, Walter, who had been promised 30,000 French francs if he kept a clean sheet. The game, such as it was, ended 1–1, though Peracio had a spectacular goal disallowed for offside. As the whistle blew for full-time, the Czech left-half, Kopecky, drove a tremendous shot against Walter's left-hand post. There were no more goals in extra time.

Two days later the teams met again, without their various casualties. Just as in the game eight years earlier in Montevideo between Chile and Argentina, violence seemed to have run its course, helped perhaps by the fact that Brazil brought in nine new players and the Czechs six. Leonidas was in magnificent form, yet many thought that though the Czech reserve keeper, Burkert, certainly played well, the mighty Planicka would have saved Leonidas's equalizer.

There were also those who thought Walter, Brazil's keeper, had scooped what looked like a good goal by Senecky back from behind the goal-line, just before Roberto, the outside-right, volleyed in the winner. Czechoslovakia, moreover, not only had to do without Nejedly's clever passing, but they also lost the excellent Kopecky, who had moved up to take his place at inside-left, twenty minutes from half-time. It would not, as we shall see, be the last outbreak of World Cup violence by a Brazilian team.

Mervyn Griffiths, the red-haired Welsh linesman (later a referee), who disallowed Puskas's equalizing goal for Hungary in the 1954 World Cup Final for offside, was to be thanked for preventing the Final Pool match of 1950 in São Paolo between Spain and Uruguay from degenerating into mayhem. 'It should be remembered,' remarked a Brazilian newspaper loftily, 'that football is a sport, not a war.'

Spain had the better of the first half, after Ghiggia had given Uruguay the lead. Even Rodriguez Andrade couldn't subdue the dashing Basora on the right wing and he scored twice. Uruguay regained control in the second half and eventually the massive Varela thundered into the penalty area to equalize, but there had been much dirty work in the interim.

This was nothing, however, compared to the problems and excesses faced by another British referee, Arthur Ellis of Yorkshire, when Brazil confronted Hungary in the quarter-finals of the 1954 World Cup in Berne.

Who began the Battle of Berne? Some said it was the Hungarians with a series of commonplace fouls, but the Hungarians' two splendid, early goals must have set the Brazilians' teeth on edge. After only three minutes, Nandor Hidegkuti, the deep-lying, opportunist centre-forward, thumped a corner from the left into the roof of the Brazilian net. He had his shorts ripped off him for his pains. Five minutes later, wearing a fresh pair of shorts and under driving rain, Hidegkuti himself crossed and up went Sandor Kocsis to nod the ball home.

The Brazilians were displeased and alarmed. They had abandoned the diagonal system of defence which had betrayed them in the decisive game of 1950 and, with Pinheiro as the stopper centre-half, were now trying to succeed with the old-style European third-back game. But it clearly wasn't natural to them, great gaps were left through lack of covering and in four years' time they'd bring to Sweden their four-in-a-line defence: two men in the middle and another four up front.

The game grew rougher. Tackling became increasingly harsh and the man was the target as often as the ball. Buzansky, one of Hungary's two large, blond full-backs, chopped down Indio, but Djalma Santos, Brazil's powerful right-back, scored from the penalty mark. Brazil were back in the game and giving as good as they got when Hungary, fifteen minutes after half-time, managed to stretch their lead again from a penalty of their own.

The second half was soon besmirched with sly fouls and deliberate obstructions, which in turn led to further penalties. Kocsis centred to Czibor, confidently taking Puskas's place at inside-left, Pinheiro handled to stop the ball reaching him, and Lantos, the other Hungarian full-back, lashed in the penalty. Now fouls were coming thick and fast, some of the nastiest behind the referee's back, but there were still moments of superb football. Julinho, the strong, fast Brazilian outside-right, a master of ball-control at speed, provided one of the most memorable of them with an astounding dribble at breakneck speed, followed by a tremendous shot wide of Gyula Grosics. Now it was 3–2 to Hungary.

The game grew rougher and rougher. Two famous and distinguished footballers, Nilton Santos, the tall elegant Brazilian left-back, and Josef Bozsik, member of the Hungarian parliament, right-half and midfield force for the national team, exchanged punches and were both sent off by Arthur Ellis. The Brazilian trainer dashed on to the field to argue with Ellis, who summoned policemen to get him off. Photographers rushed on in their turn and still more policemen.

The game, if you could call it that, resumed. There was a fearful moment when Djalma Santos, spitting and threatening, was chasing Czibor round the field, behind Arthur Ellis's back. Eventually, when there were just four minutes left to play, Ellis sent off another Brazilian – Humberto Tozzi, who fell to his knees pleading not to go. But go he did, with tears rolling down his cheeks. A minute later, Czibor crossed, Kocsis headed and the Hungarians scored their fourth goal.

That was the end of the scoring, with Hungary winning 4–2, but it was, alas, by no means the end of the violence.

As the teams left the field, Pinheiro, passing the Hungarian bench, was struck on the head with a bottle. Was it Ferenc Puskas, the injured Hungarian captain? One leading Italian newspaper believed it was, so did Ernst Thommen, the Swiss President of the

World Cup Committee, who announced that he would be presenting a full report, having himself been present when the Brazilians attacked the Hungarians in their dressing room after the game. For some reason, the report was never made. The match, which could and should have been a splendid one, goes down as one of the most squalid in the history of the World Cup – and Ellis as one of its bravest referees.

The game might well have been described as uncontrollable – the word used by another English referee, the Ilford schoolmaster, Ken Aston, after the fearful Battle of Santiago between Chile and Italy in 1962.

Before a ball was even kicked there was bad blood between the two countries, who were due to meet in the second game of their eliminating group. Two Italian journalists had written highly critical articles about life and customs in Santiago, the Chilean capital, which had been angrily reproduced and attacked in the Santiago Press.

The atmosphere in the new national stadium was fearsome from the start. The Italian players later complained that the Chileans were spitting in their faces and insulting them almost as soon as they came on to the field. Who was to blame? Italian reporters accused their own players of being too easily provoked. *L'Équipe* of Paris wrote: 'The feebleness of the English referee, Mr Aston, who never succeeded in hiding his lack of authority beneath an imperturbable front and who was too conscious of "the voice of the people", succeeded in transforming a lively match into a veritable street fight.'

But it was not entirely Aston's fault, particularly as he wasn't given an ounce of support by his linesmen, who unquestionably saw a number of things which happened off the ball behind his back, but chose not to tell him. It was behind Aston's back, for example, that Leonel Sanchez, the Chilean left-winger, punched Maschio, Italy's Argentine-born inside-right, with a left hook, breaking his nose. A scene witnessed by millions again and again on the television. So Sanchez didn't get sent off, Maschio was rendered useless for the rest of the game, and the only two players expelled were Italians.

Ferrini went after only seven minutes for chopping down the

centre-forward, Landa, and David, who took a retaliatory kick at Leonel Sanchez's head, was sent off shortly afterwards. It was no real wonder that Italy, virtually reduced to eight sound men, should go down 2–0; if anything it was more surprising that they resisted until fifteen minutes before the end when Ramirez headed in Leonel Sanchez's free-kick. A second goal was scored by the capable, hard-shooting Toro, in the very last minute.

In 1966, as we have seen, there were the Argentine excesses, their captain Rattin being sent off at Wembley in the quarter-finals by the tiny German referee Herr Kreitlein for what he described as 'the look on his face'. But the worst incidents of all took place the same day at Sheffield in the match between West Germany and Uruguay.

The crisis came when the Uruguayans claimed and believed, when they were 1–0 down to a lucky deflected goal by Haller, that Karl-Heinz Schnellinger had handled on the goal-line. When Lothar Emmerich, the German left-winger, kicked the big Uruguayan skipper, Troche, painfully, it was war. Troche retaliated at once by kicking him in the stomach, he was sent off by Jim Finney, the English referee, and slapped Seeler's face on the way for good measure. That was five minutes after half-time, another five minutes and a second Uruguayan, the inside-left Silva, was expelled for chopping down Haller.

Haller, indeed, was one of the chief victims of this unpleasant afternoon: one Uruguayan grabbed him so cruelly and painfully that he collapsed in agony and was oozing blood that evening. So much for those who accused him and other Germans of merely being bad actors.

By the World Cup of 1974, the Uruguayans, who twenty years earlier had figured in one of the finest, most sporting games ever seen in the competition, when they lost the semi-final to Hungary in Lausanne, were notorious for their thuggery. On a pre-World-Cup tour of Australia, one of their defenders had struck the Australian centre-forward on the side of the neck with a karate blow and paralysed him. But the worst piece of violence of the 1974 World Cup would concern the Haitians and would happen off the field.

Ernst Jean-Joseph, Haiti's red-haired centre-half, played a sturdy game against Italy in Munich, but was then found to have taken a stimulant beforehand. He claimed it was for his asthma. Few believed him. He was suspended at once, dragged out of the sports centre at Grunwals by sinister Haitian officials – members, it was said, of the terrifying Tons-Tons Macoute's secret police – beaten, shoved into a car, locked up in a room at the Sheraton Hotel and flown back to Haiti the next morning. Fortunately, the poor, terrified young man did not disappear in Haiti like Larry Gaetjens, scorer of America's 1950 goal against England, had. He lived to play again ... in America.

8 ● World Cup Wingers

Wingers are important. A rare breed of player and one that should be preserved. We very nearly saw the last of them after England's wingless wonders won the 1966 World Cup, yet the history of the tournament is rich in marvellous outside-rights and lefts: Chico Ghiggia, Abbadie and Borges of Uruguay, Julinho, Garrincha and Jairzinho of Brazil, Stanley Matthews and Tom Finney of England, Helmut Rahn of West Germany, Bruno Conti, Raimondo Orsi, Guaita and Biavati of Italy, and Lato and Gadocha of Poland. A winger is something special. No one else can do quite what he does, least of all an attacking, overlapping full-back. A winger is the only player who can tempt the opposing full-back on to the wrong foot with a body swerve, flick the ball past him down the touchline and carry on to deliver the most dangerous pass of all: the ball pulled back across the face of the defence to forwards lurking eagerly for the kill.

Stanley Matthews had perfected the art. When Tom Finney came along, and later Garrincha, it became fashionable to criticize him, to say that Finney and Garrincha could do all that Matthews did and more. I saw them all play. I have seen all the best Brazilian wingers since the war. I saw Lato and Gadocha strike terror into opponents with their famous double act in 1974; I saw Ghiggia, a spent force, a lost figure, in Rome only four years after his wonderful World Cup in Rio; and I watched Stan Matthews from 1942, on the England right wing at Wembley, until he retired, aged fifty, in 1965. Let me assure you that there has never been a player like him.

He would no doubt have played in the 1938 World Cup had England accepted the invitation to enter. As it was, he had to wait until 1950 when he got only one game, England's last, against Spain in Rio, when it was just too late for him to put things right. He played splendidly in 1954 in Switzerland at the age of thirty-nine. Two years later at Wembley I saw him dance delightful rings around the big Brazilian left-back, Nilton Santos who, for the next two World Cups, would put wingers – even Sweden's Hamrin – in his pocket. Matthews was forty-one at the time and he said to me afterwards that there were times when, reading that he was allegedly too old to go on, he 'could tear the paper across'. I didn't blame him.

As we have seen, in 1950 Matthews was called up for the England World Cup team in Brazil only at the very last moment, which was absolutely typical of the way he was treated throughout his long and great career. Born on 1 February, 1915, in the Potteries at Hanley, Matthews joined Stoke City straight from school as the office boy. He quickly got into the first team and at the age of nineteen won his first couple of caps for England.

The second of them came in the notorious Battle of Highbury against the violent Italian World Cup winning team that November, 1934. Geoffrey Simpson, sports columnist of the *Daily Mail*, criticized Matthews for showing 'the same faults of slowness and hesitation' as in his debut against Wales. 'Perhaps,' he concluded fatuously, 'he lacks the big match temperament.' As the next thirty-one years would show, Matthews was nothing if not a great occasion player; indeed the greater the occasion, the more formidable he became.

But the England selectors were never quite sure of him. His original, eccentric ways baffled them and they tended to leave him out when they could. His control, his feathery body swerve, were wonderful to watch. Everybody knew exactly what he was going to do, but still there was hardly a left-back who could stop him as his body swayed inside, put them on the wrong foot, and as with a flick and spurt he went past them away up the wing. 'Don't ask me how I do it,' he once said plaintively to an inquirer, 'it just comes out of me under pressure.'

During the war his Air Force duties took him to Blackpool. He played for the Lancashire seaside club as a guest and after the war left Stoke to join them. Later, in 1961, Blackpool made a generous gesture, selling him back to Stoke for a token fee. Thus he returned to the Potteries in his final years and promptly helped Stoke to get back into the First Division.

Tom Finney was much younger than Matthews, but emerged to challenge him in the 1940s as a right-winger. By 1941 he was already a young star in his local Preston North End team, but was then sent abroad by the Army. Reports of his marvellous talents came back from the Middle East where he won the admiration of a once great Scottish outside-right, Alec Jackson. On his return, Finney, a natural left-footer playing on the right, with exquisite footwork, supreme balance and outstanding intelligence, at first displaced Matthews.

But in Lisbon in May, 1947, the ideal compromise was found. Matthews was brought back to play on the right, Finney played on the left and Portugal were thrashed – 10–0! The same combination proved equally formidable in 1948 when Italy were beaten 4–0 in Turin, Finney scoring two of the goals and Matthews going round poor Eliani, Italy's reserve left-back, as if he wasn't there. Three years later the same combination was tried again against Spain in Rio.

Both Finney and Matthews played excellent games in Rio, with their clever control and pace – Matthews never seemed to lose his amazing spurt, after beating the back. Chances were made, but the English forwards didn't take them, save on one occasion when Jackie Milburn scored, but was given rather dubiously offside. The only goal of the match was headed by the Spanish centre-forward, Zarra; Ramallet's fine keeping kept the English out and England were eliminated. The question of whether the Matthews–Finney combination would have demolished the United States in Belo Horizonte remained unanswered.

In 1954, Matthews, in a glorious display against Belgium, showed that he was perfectly capable of moving off his wing and playing a much more central part in the game. People tended to forget that he had already shown as much at Tottenham in 1938, when he played for England against the clever Czech team. Jack Crayston, the England right-half, had been hurt and Matthews, moving to inside-right, had saved England's bacon with a splendid hat-trick, scoring every goal with his *left* foot. England had won 5–4.

As in 1950, Matthews was brought back to the England team for the Swiss World Cup at the last moment, having been dropped for some time. He had not figured in the side humiliated 7–1 in Budapest by Puskas and the Hungarians, just before the tournament.

In Basel, Matthews was England's undoubted star against the Belgians, until he pulled a muscle in extra time. Sometimes he was on the right wing, but later in the game he was more often off it than not, sometimes flowing past four or five players at a time. One of his dribbles gave the inside-right, Ivor Broadis, a goal; then Tom Finney, sent down the left by Tommy Taylor, crossed for the Bolton centre-forward, Nat Lofthouse, to hurl himself at the ball and head another goal.

But though England held a 3–1 lead until the final quarter of an hour, they just could not master Rik Coppens, the sturdy Belgian centre-forward. Their lead was wiped out and in the end they had to concede a draw when their left-half, Jimmy Dickinson, headed past Gil Merrick, the English goalkeeper, whose inadequacy had been quite obvious since the previous November, when Hungary beat him six times at Wembley.

Matthews missed the next game against Switzerland, won 2–0 in Berne, but Finney ably took his place on the right. Then Matthews came back for the quarter-final, played in torrid heat in Basel against the holders, Uruguay. It was an exciting game, with England three times behind, fighting back desperately and eventually going down 4–2. 'Matt–ews! Matt–ews!' chanted an enthusiastic Swiss crowd as the maestro sent Denis Wilshaw through the middle with a perfectly angled pass, cleverly taking Varela out of the game and making the equalizer for Nat Lofthouse: 1–1. Sometimes a besieged Uruguay had eight men back in their defence, yet despite the fact that Varela, Abbadie and Andrade were all injured, Merrick's porous goalkeeping let England down, though at 3–2 to Uruguay a rampant Matthews would hit the post.

That was his last World Cup, though Finney would play a solitary game in Gothenburg against the Russians in 1958. As for the Uruguayans, their 1954 wingers were even better than those of 1950.

Julio Abbadie on the right and Carlos Borges on the left tore the Scottish defence to pieces in their second game in Basel. Borges

above left Johan Cruyff, superb striker and masterly inspiration of the Dutch team in 1974.

above right Eusebio Ferreira Da Silva, probably the best Portuguese international forward of all time and leading scorer of the 1966 tournament with nine goals.

below Paolo Rossi (*left*), Italian hero of the 1982 World Cup, evades an Aston Villa defender.

Tom Finney, the Preston outside-left and arguably superior even to Matthews, volleys for goal.

Stanley Matthews, the most legendary outside-right in the history of British football, was always leaving defenders trailing in his wake.

Gordon Banks, England's goalkeeper, dives to save from A. Spencer, Uruguay's centre-forward, in the opening match of the 1966 World Cup tournament.

England beat the Rest of the World, 1963. Yachine, the Russian goalkeeper for the Rest, dives to take the ball from the feet of Jimmy Greaves, England's inside-left.

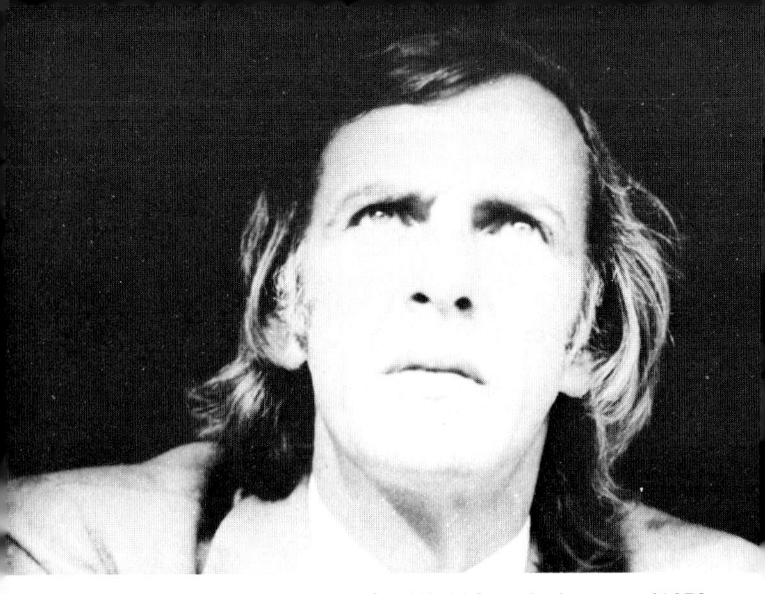

Cesar Luis Menotti, manager of the World Cup winning team of 1978.

below left West Germany's captain and sweeper, Franz Beckenbauer, holding the World Cup aloft in 1974.

below right Bobby Moore, international left-half, who captained England to World Cup success at Wembley in 1966 and was named Player of the tournament, seen here playing for Fulham in the latter years of his career.

Alf Ramsey training with the England team at Stanmore in 1963, soon after he took over as manager.

The 1966 World Cup team with the World Cup. *Back row from right to left:* Harold Shepherdson (trainer), Nobby Stiles, Roger Hunt, Gordon Banks, Jack Charlton, George Cohen, Ray Wilson, Alf Ramsey. *Front row from right to left:* Martin Peters, Geoff Hurst, Bobby Moore, Alan Ball, Bobby Charlton.

Geoff Hurst, one of the heroes of England's triumph in the 1966 World Cup Final, scores again.

Pelé, perhaps the finest player of all time, here aged seventeen, scores his third goal for Brazil in the semi-final against France in Stockholm, 1958.

Italy's goalkeeper and captain, Dino Zoff, saves from Socrates of Brazil, 1982.

Bobby Charlton, England's outside-left, has the Mexican defence in a tangle as he tries to break through and score another goal in the match at Wembley Stadium, 1961, in which England beat Mexico 8–0.

Master of the ball, Argentinian Diego Maradona is sent crashing to the ground by the German, Stielike, 1982.

Michel Platini of France (here in the Juventus strip) displaying his dribbling, 'cutting as the blade of a knife'.

scored 3, Abbadie 2, and the final tally was 7–0 to Uruguay, leaving the Scottish defence, as one unkind English critic had it, 'standing around like Highland cattle'.

The Scots had not played badly in their opening game against the Austrians, losing only 1–0, with Schmied in the Austrian goal being kept far busier than Fred Martin. Ominously, Martin had only been chosen after a lot of goalkeeper trouble – an all too familiar story with Scotland.

Why did the Scots collapse against Uruguay? The resignation after the first game of Andy Beattie, their former left-back, then team manager, incensed by interference from his officials, may have had something to do with it. Pipers in kilts did their best to inspire Scotland, but apparently without effect.

Juan Schiaffino, in wonderful form at inside-left for Uruguay, controlled the entire game. Later, Tommy Docherty would say he was the greatest inside-forward he had ever played against, including Ferenc Puskas. The final goal, Uruguay's seventh, scored by Abbadie ten minutes from the end, epitomized Uruguay's total superiority. He dribbled round both Scottish full-backs, Aird and Cunningham, and then Martin for good measure, before tapping home.

Zoltan Czibor of Hungary, that famous left-winger, played his best football of the tournament when deputizing for Puskas at inside-left, revelling in the extra work; while, as we know, it was a winger, the hefty Helmut Rahn, who scored two goals for West Germany, including the winner against Hungary, in the rain-soaked Final.

Rahn would be there again four years later in Sweden where the Swedes themselves had an electric pair of wingers in Kurt (Kurre) Hamrin and Lennart (Nacka) Skoglund, formidable in all but the Final, when the big Santoses of Brazil just snuffed them out.

Hamrin and Skoglund dribbled and dashed superbly, giving edge, pace and bite to a somewhat elderly Swedish team. Both were then with Italian clubs. They provided some of the most exciting moments of the 1958 World Cup, though when Skoglund reacted angrily to Hungarian provocation in an early game in Stockholm, little George Raynor, who had launched his World Cup career eight years earlier in Brazil, announced that he'd be talking to him in the morning: 'We want no circus men in our team.'

The so-called circus man had cleverly made Sweden's first goal, beating his opponent twice before crossing for Hamrin to score. Hamrin later beat Grosics for the second goal with a deflected lob. Hamrin, who was brought to Italy by Juventus, lent to Padova because Juventus couldn't find room for him and eventually joined Fiorentina where he played for nine years with enormous success, was tremendously effective. Small, well-made, with a low centre of gravity, great dribbling and finishing ability and habitually wearing his socks around his ankles, he was a terribly difficult man to stop.

In the quarter-finals, against a weary but determined Russian team in Stockholm, exhausted by their play-off against England, Hamrin was a one-man *Blitzkrieg*. Twice, despite his lack of height, he almost headed a goal; in the end, after he had made the run and put in the cross, he did manage to head it in when the ball bounced loose. A couple of minutes from time, he switched wings and put across a ball from the left-hand goal-line which was knocked home by the young, blond centre-forward, Agne Simonsson.

It was in the Gothenburg semi-final against West Germany, however, that Hamrin scored what was surely the goal of his life and one which can be classed alongside Pelé's as among the best of the 1958 World Cup. True, what went before it was not wholly pleasing. Hamrin had been running Juskowiak, the German left-back, ragged. Finally, Juskowiak took a kick at his tormentor who rolled over and over as if poleaxed. As soon as Juskowiak had been sent off, however, Hamrin recovered with remarkable speed. Certainly no seriously injured player could ever have got the kind of goal he did. He had already helped create the goal, nine minutes from time, with which Gunnar Gren shot Sweden coolly into a 2–1 lead, Hamrin's own shot having been blocked. Then came his own astonishing goal. First, stopping dead with the ball, he walked it almost distractedly towards the right touchline. Suddenly and electrically, he came to life, turning inside with the ball, spinning and sprinting past three defenders and finally shooting past Herkenrath in the German goal.

The Final, however, would belong to Garrincha.

You might say Garrincha was a child of nature, for many playing years a happy innocent; his later years were very unhappy, however, and he died a wretched, early death in 1983. He came from the village of Pau Grande in the state of Rio, and though christened Michael Francisco dos Santos, he was always known by his nickname, Garrincha, the name of a small bird. He was born crippled and though his left leg was eventually made serviceable – wonderfully so – it was always twisted and distorted. In a curious way, this may have been the secret of his amazing body swerve, his ability to go outside opponents and down the right-hand touchline at sudden phenomenal speed. Certainly he was a terribly hard man to play against.

Brazil took him to Sweden in 1958, but he didn't play in the first two games. Vicente Feola, the big-bellied, rumbling manager, had little time for Garrincha's undisciplined style and preferred to use the Flamengo winger, Joel, in an attack which had initially had four Flamengo players.

After the 0–0 draw with England in Gothenburg, however, in which England could easily have been given a penalty when Kevan was brought down, the Brazilian players realized something would have to be done. A deputation of them, led by the left-back, Nilton Santos, Garrincha's club mate at Botafogo of Rio, went to Feola and begged him to include Garrincha in the game against Russia. Feola agreed.

As the teams lined up for the national anthem in the Ullevi Stadium, Gothenburg, Nilton whispered to Garrincha that he mustn't let them down. But Garrincha scarcely listened. He was laughing. 'Look at that linesman there,' he said, 'he looks just like Charlie Chaplin!'

Once the game began, however, Garrincha was irrestible. He turned the left-back inside out, 'reduced him to shredded Russian cabbage', as a Scottish reporter picturesquely put it, and in the opening minutes swerved past him with ease to drive a shot against the left-hand post. Poor Kuznetsov never got near Garrincha in the game, which Brazil won 2–0, and towards the end, Garrincha amused himself by holding on to the ball despite the efforts of five Russian defenders. It was a memorable moment.

Mel Hopkins of Wales gave him a good game in the quarter-final at Gothenburg, but in the Final Garrincha showed how formidably effective he could be. Sweden took an early lead through Nils Liedholm, but six minutes later Zito, the attacking right-half, found Garrincha on the right wing. Off he went with an amazing, dynamic burst of speed, swerving outside Parling and Axbom, the Swedish defenders, then pulling the ball back for Vavà who came hurtling in to drive it past Svensson.

Thirteen minutes from half-time the same thing happened again. Garrincha left the Swedish left flank standing, pulled the ball back and Vavà thundered in to do execution. Thus by half-time Brazil had turned a 1–0 deficit into a 2–1 lead and in the second half, as their overjoyed fans, careless of the rain, chanted, 'Samba, samba!' they danced home to a 5–2 victory.

If Garrincha was an outstandingly decisive player in 1958, he was still more remarkable four years later in Chile when, with Pelé dropping out after the second game, he rose to heights of versatility and skill, not to say goal-scoring ability, of which no one would have suspected him capable, even in Stockholm. There seemed to be nothing he could not do. Though only a little fellow, five feet seven inches in height, he actually outjumped the towering England centre-half, Maurice Norman, to head a goal from a corner in the quarter-final game in Viña del Mar. A natural right-footer, he struck shots with his left that Puskas might have envied, while his right foot swerved in devastating shots and free-kicks that became the terror of near-sighted goalkeepers such as Ron Springett.

When Brazil beat Spain in their third game at Viña del Mar, they had Garrincha to thank. With four minutes left, the score was 1–1 and Spain had been the better team. Then Garrincha broke away in one of his famous swerves and bursts, crossed, and Amarildo, Pelé's deputy, raced in to head the winner.

Against England, on the same ground, Garrincha was extraordinary. There was nothing even a left-back as quick, strong and mobile as Ray Wilson could do with him. Indeed, there was nothing the England team at large could do with him.

He headed the first, remarkable goal, as we have seen, for Brazil. England equalized when Gerry Hitchens, their centre-forward, headed against the Brazilian bar and Jimmy Greaves, in one of his few notable moments of the tournament, tapped in. But in the second half Garrincha decided the game with two ferocious, swerving, long shots. The first, from a free-kick, completely deceived Ron Springett, bouncing off his chest for Vavà to score. Later Garrincha made it 3–1 with another astonishing shot, one which again totally deceived Springett. It was a diabolical swerving tag shot and seemed to be going outside the right-hand post, then suddenly at the last moment it curled to finish just inside it and in the net.

In the semi-final against Chile in Santiago, Garrincha was just as devastating. Indeed, scornful of the huge home crowd's ecstatic zeal, he seemed determined to beat Chile on his own. After only nine minutes, from an inside-left position some twenty yards out, he spun to hit a searing left-footed shot, which ripped past Chile's goalkeeper, Escutti, giving Brazil the lead. He then made it 2–0 with another staggering leap to Zagalo's corner, crowned by a fierce header. Chile got a goal back, but a characteristic effort by Brazil's other famous winger, Zagalo, who tricked his man, delivered a short centre which was headed in by Vavà, restored the two-goal lead.

Towards the end of the game Garrincha, who had been given much rough treatment by Rojas, retaliated with a kick and was sent off. As he went round the track a bottle struck him and cut open his head.

So to the Final. Would Garrincha be allowed to play? Normally he would have been suspended automatically, but the President of Brazil, who was said to have listened to the semi-final commentary on headphones during Mass, personally sent a cable of appeal. Garrincha was allowed to play, but curiously, after all his wonderful moments in the previous games, he had a subdued afternoon.

Indeed, one's chief memory of him, late in the game when Brazil were winning 3–1 and clearly had the Cup in their pockets, is of him bringing the ball up to Popluhar, the huge, half-Czech centre-half, shimmying and swerving, while Popluhar put his hands on his hips in massive disdain as if to say, 'Haven't you done enough?'

A motor accident, as well as the passing of the years, seriously affected Garrincha's form in the run-up to the 1966 World Cup in England. Dr Hilton Gosling, the big medical adviser to the Brazilian team, whose expert knowledge and calm personality had done so much for their success, said before the tournament that Garrincha had recovered from his injuries, but not completely. 'The problem with Garrincha is this: he can't play as often as he used to play because his recovery is quite slow now.' The Brazilian selectors foolishly ignored this.

After the opening match against Bulgaria at Everton, in which he scored Brazil's second goal from one of his typical, bending free-kicks, Garrincha was shoved into the next match against Hungary when he was plainly far from ready. Needless to say, he did little in what proved to be his last World Cup match, but it was no longer the real Garrincha playing.

Zagalo was no longer playing at all. A very different type of player from Garrincha, equally talented but far less spectacular and explosive, he was more of a thoughtful player than an instinctive one and he would become a World Cup winning manager as well as being twice a World Cup winning player.

Zagalo's chief attribute apart from skill and tactical sense was his amazing stamina. He was said to have built it by swimming among the breakers in the north of Brazil – he was tireless. This he proved in the World Cup Final of 1958: in the first half he dropped so deep that he was there to head the ball off his own goal-line; later, with thirteen minutes left, he picked his way skilfully past Boerjesson and the big right-back, Bergmark, to shoot past Svensson for Brazil's fifth goal – at which he knelt on the ground weeping tears of sheer joy. He was clearly not quite the cool, calm figure he might have seemed.

It was thanks to Zagalo's energy and all-round ability that, when Pelé was hurt in Chile, Brazil were able to turn their 4-2-4 formation into 4-3-3. They had shown a tendency towards it even in Sweden, where Zagalo had, when necessary, always been ready and able to drop back to help his defence.

From this you may see that 4-3-3, which proceeded to sweep most of the game just as 4-2-4 had done, was born not so much on the drawing board as on the playing field: the natural response to particular events – chiefly the loss of Pelé. If you had a player with Zagalo's energy, versatility and skill, you could make 4-3-3 work superbly. Indeed, you might say that Zagalo was the forerunner of the kind of winger future managers were to look for: players who did not just stand out on the flank waiting for the ball, but dropped back to get it and to help their own full-backs, as the talented Steve Coppell would later do for Manchester United and England in the 1982 World Cup and as Bruno Conti would so successfully do for Italy in the same competition.

Conti, indeed, set up the third Italian goal in the 1982 World Cup Final against West Germany in Madrid. When Briegel was brought down in the Italian penalty area, Conti ran from deep in his own half to the German box, then pulled the ball across the middle for the lanky Altobelli to score with ease.

Garrincha was the second of three superb Brazilian outside-rights. The first was Julinho, with his power, pace, close control and hugely accurate and forceful right-footed shooting. Like Hamrin, he went off to play on the right wing in Florence for Fiorentina, helping them to win the Championship. He later returned to play brilliantly for Brazil, though never in another World Cup.

After Garrincha came Jairzinho, a winger very much in the same mould, though in fact he preferred to play centre-forward for Botafogo, Garrincha's old club in Rio, and played the same position in the World Cup of 1974. His finest World Cup came in Mexico in 1970, when his dashing, muscular play gave perfect balance to Brazil's superb attack.

In Guadalajara against Czechoslovakia he began as he meant to go on, scoring Brazil's third and fourth goals with characteristic bursts of tremendous strength and speed. Trying to stop Jairzinho on the break was like trying to stop a tank. For the first of those goals, driven home with his tremendous right foot at the end of a run, he may have started from an offside position, but there could be absolutely no doubt about his second, Brazil's fourth. It was a remarkable feat – he shook off no fewer than three Czech defenders, one of whom tried unsuccessfully to foul him, before shooting past Viktor into the net.

It was Jairzinho, too, who was England's downfall in the next game; he who broke clear of a helpless left-back, Terry Cooper, and put the ball on Pelé's head for Banks to make that marvellous save; and he who shot past the goalkeeper in the second half, after Pelé's smooth lay-off in the goalmouth.

Against Rumania, Jairzinho scored his fourth goal of the competition when the other clever winger, Paolo Cesar, got to the left-hand goal-line and pulled the ball back. He even got Brazil's fourth goal against Peru in the quarter-final from Tostão's pass, despite being ill on that day. And there was nothing the matter with him when it came to the semi-final against Uruguay, when he scored another of his rampaging goals, Brazil's second, in the second half, taking a pass (again) from Tostão, roaring past the much slower, less powerful Mujica with ease, and shooting home.

In the Final against Italy at the huge Aztec Stadium in Mexico City, he varied his game, taking most people by surprise. Giacinto Facchetti, the huge Italian left-back famous for his overlapping play, was no exception. He had expected Jairzinho to stay out on the wing and attack from there; instead Jairzinho kept moving inside, pulling the unhappy Facchetti all over the place and thereby creating great gaps on the right flank into which Brazil's attacking right-back and captain, Carlos Alberto, could move. Both scored goals in the second half, first Jairzinho then Alberto, driving home balls thoughtfully laid off to them by the clever Pelé.

In the 1974 tournament Jairzinho did his energetic best as centre-forward in a Brazilian team greatly inferior to that of 1970. He missed a very good chance to put them ahead against Holland in the rain at Dortmund, before the Dutch scored twice in the second half and won to reach the Final.

In 1970 the succession of great Brazilian outside-rights had looked as if it would go on for ever. Instead it simply faded out, as did the long line of great Brazilian centre-forwards. In the 1974, 1978 and 1982 tournaments, Brazil's lack of an exceptional right-winger was sadly evident. Not even their dazzling four-man midfield in Spain could make up for the lack of talent at the front.

In the late 1960s and 1970s there was a definite tendency for wingers, however naturally gifted, to prefer to come off the wing and play a more central role. We have seen it in the case of Jairzinho. It was also true much earlier of Tom Finney, for he concluded his distinguished career with Preston as a deep-lying centre-forward in the Kopa style, using his balance, his ability to beat opponents and his skilled passing to run the whole attack. His injury in the first match against Russia in Gothenburg in 1958 had put the last nail in England's coffin, for there was no one who could possibly have taken his place, and Bryan Douglas of Blackburn on the other wing, a little player of immense talent, was tired and ineffectual.

Four years later Douglas would play on the England right wing in Chile, scoring a clever goal against Argentina in Rancagua, but he too would eventually move to the middle, becoming a skilled, constructive inside-left.

Gigi Riva of Italy was another dissatisfied winger. Foolishly and surprisingly, despite a number of impressive games, Italy left him out of their 1966 World Cup team in England. Originally a left-winger with Legnano in the north, he had made his name with Cagliari on the island of Sardinia, inspiring that team not only to the First Division, but also to win the Championship. Twice he broke a leg and twice he recovered. He was fast, strong and direct. He had a magnificent left-footed shot with which in 1968 he scored one of the goals whereby Italy beat Yugoslavia in Rome in the replayed Nations Cup Final.

By 1970 and the eve of the first Mexican World Cup, Riva had become an idol, a magical figure whose very name produced applause and whose goals would take Italy to glory and the title. In the event he did not really come to life until the quarter-finals partly, perhaps, because the Italians were so drearily defensive, particularly in the early phases, and partly too, no doubt, because of the immense weight of expectation put on him by the Italian public. One almost had the impression he was expected to win the Cup on his own. The Italians also suffered from what might be called a North Korean complex. Italy were terrified of another devastating defeat such as that of 1966.

Having scraped into the quarter-finals with a minimum of decent football, the Italians finally came out of their shell in the quarter-finals against Mexico at Toluca. In the second half, little Gianni Rivera of Milan came on as substitute for his rival Sandrino Mazzola of Internazionale, the other Milanese club, and proceeded to inspire the Italian team.

Now Gigi Riva really cut loose. With the score at 1–1 at half-time, Rivera exchanged passes with the other skilled inside-forward, Picchio De Sisti, and crossed to Riva. Riva thundered past two defenders in his best style, then, though the angle was tight, beat the Mexican keeper, Calderon, to put Italy ahead. Riva's next shot was blocked, as was Domenghini's, but Rivera scored and the fourth Italian goal went again to Riva, sent through by another delightful pass from Rivera.

Though Italy scored four goals in the semi-final against West Germany, Riva scored only one of them. It was a typical piece of powerful opportunism, a goal made out of virtually nothing. In the first period of extra time with the score at 2–2, Riva pivoted sharply out on the left to beat Schnellinger, then drove in a low and ferocious left-footed cross shot.

The World Cup Final held in the same Aztec Stadium should have been Riva's stage, yet he was hardly to be seen. Italy played a pitifully cautious, fear-ridden, negative game, losing 4–1. Of all their forwards only Roberto Boninsegna, who scored their equalizing goal just before half-time, did himself real justice.

Riva figured, after a fashion, in the 1974 World Cup, but by then he was clearly past his best. He played against Haiti in Munich, hardly played against Argentina in Stuttgart, and was brusquely dropped from Italy's last game.

The strange irony of the Italy v. Argentina game was that Italy had got themselves into such a bewildering tactical mess that they should have been torn to pieces for the first twenty minutes by the classic Argentine winger, little René Houseman.

For some unknown reason, Valcareggi, the Italian manager, decided that Houseman was going to play in midfield – an extraordinary assumption when you consider his particular gifts of balance, pace and control. Indeed, it would seem impossible to regard Houseman as anything but a two-footed winger. Valcareggi none the less set his own creative inside-forward, Fabio Capello, to mark him. Houseman ran circles round Capello for a full twenty minutes before the Italians woke up to Valcareggi's mistake which had turned Capello into a full-back. Though by this time Houseman had already shot the Argentines into the lead. Italy then put the fearsome Romeo Benetti on to him, gradually came back into the game and eventually equalized. But they went down – and out – to the splendid Poland team, which included Lato and Gadocha.

They were a deadly pair. Lato on the right wing, Gadocha on the left, they came together only when Lubanski, the star inside-left and captain of the Polish team, was hurt playing against England in Katowice in 1973. Gadocha, a tough, fast, clever outside-left with a powerful left foot, was already well installed, but room was now made for Lato on the right in the first of his three distinguished World Cups. In 1974 Lato still had plenty of pace, in addition to excellent control and a keen tactical sense; it was the combination of Lato and Gadocha that made Poland so powerful.

The Poles prevented a surprised England from qualifying for the 1974 finals by holding them to a draw at Wembley. During this goal-less draw, Lato would undoubtedly have scored a marvellous solo goal, having run half the length of the field, had not the English centre-half, Roy McFarland, disgracefully held him back with an arm round his neck. Lato was a very hard man to stop and Gadocha a hard man to come up against, as the Welsh would find in Katowice. In Cardiff the Welsh had kicked the Poles out of the game and beaten them; in Katowice the Poles retaliated with savage interest, Gadocha once clearly butting an opponent.

Already in the opening game against Argentina in West Germany, their direct involvement in all three Polish goals had shown what a dangerous partnership they were. Two of these goals came in the seventh minute, when Carnevali, the fallible Argentine keeper, dropped Gadocha's corner, Lato immediately put it in the net; then, with a beautiful pass, Lato split Argentina's square defence for the brisk new centre-forward, Szarmach, to score. Argentina belatedly and successfully introduced little Houseman, socks around his ankles, for the second half, but there was still a third Polish goal to come. When Carnevali carelessly threw the ball straight at Lato's feet, he didn't hesitate, he simply raced straight through and scored. Babington got a late goal after hitting the post of an open goal and 3–2 was the final margin of victory.

Lato and Gadocha ran riot in Poland's 7–0 victory over Haiti, Lato getting two of the goals. Poland then beat Italy 2–1 and so went through to the second round where they won their first two games against Sweden and Yugoslavia respectively, but with little to spare. They were lucky to beat Sweden in Stuttgart – the Swedes had much the better of the early play, but then missed two fine chances and a penalty and paid the price when the deadly combination of Lato and Gadocha struck. Gadocha, goal maker now rather than goal scorer, crossed from the left, Szarmach got his head to the ball and Lato headed it past the agile Hellstroem.

Next came Yugoslavia in Frankfurt. Deyna, the inspiration of the Polish team now that Lubanski had gone and allowed him space to grow and flourish, opened the scoring from a penalty, recklessly given away by Karasi, who then brilliantly equalized. But the deadly pair struck yet again. This time Gadocha took a corner, Lato met the ball on the near post with a header and in it went. As we know, it took an astonishing double save by Maier on the same, now waterlogged, Frankfurt pitch to deny Poland, Lato and Gadocha a place in the Final.

Lato was there again in Argentina in 1978 but without Gadocha, and resourceful though Lato still was, it just wasn't the same. He got the only goal of the game in Rosario against a brave Tunisian side, three minutes from half-time, showing his old ability to capitalize on the opposition's mistakes, in this case Jebali's. Then Poland beat Mexico 3–1 and Poland were through to the second round.

They had a fine chance to win, or certainly to draw, against Argentina in Rosario, but failed. Argentina were 1–0 ahead when Lato drove in a shot which beat the keeper, Fillol, but Mario Kempes, who had put his team ahead and would eventually score its second goal, popped up in a different, more decisive if less pleasing role. He punched the ball off the line and Deyna, alas, missed the penalty.

Lato would score again in Poland's third match of the pool in Mendoza against Brazil, but the Brazilians won 3–1 and so Poland went out. It was Argentina who qualified.

Four years later in Spain, Lato was there again. But if things had been different and more difficult for him in Argentina where Poland kept only himself and Szarmach upfield, they were practically impossible now. Boniek had been suspended and Poland foolishly asked Lato to take his place against Italy in the semi-final, moving him back upfield to his old right-wing position despite his advanced age. Earlier in the tournament, playing in midfield, he had often looked very good indeed, sometimes breaking through from deep positions down his old, familiar right wing in a way which summoned up the past. He was a winger no more, but he was an excellent midfielder, playing in Belgium, but glad to be recalled to the colours.

He had a magnificent second half against Peru in Galicia, breaking the deadlock of draws in Poland's group, inspiring his team to five goals and a 5–1 win and scoring once himself.

It was Lato too, playing his hundredth game for Poland, who made the crucial opening goal after only three minutes in Barcelona, against the Belgians. He pulled the ball across the penalty area in his best 1974 style and Zbigniew Boniek, the red-haired inside-forward, playing as a striker, crashed in it. In Boniek's own words, this 'killed the Belgians and they just lost control of the game'. Boniek, bound for Juventus of Turin, had already distinguished himself four years earlier in Argentina, after a foolish reluctance by the team manager, Gmoch, to select him. Stupidly he got himself suspended from the semi-final, but the idea of playing Lato up front beside the exciting new left winger, Smolarek, didn't work at all and Boniek's value was proved.

It was sad that Lato should bow out of the World Cup on such a note, but over the three tournaments he had unquestionably established himself as one of the most effective players in World Cup history, particularly when in partnership with Gadocha.

He was certainly outshone, however, in the semi-final at Nou Camp, by the little Italian winger, Bruno Conti. Like Johan Neeskens of Holland, Conti, who was born at Nettuno on the Mediterranean coast, was initially interested in baseball. Turned down by Roma and Juventus, he was launched by Anzio's fine youth coach, Domenico Biti, nicknamed 'the Magician of the Mediterranean'. Roma were lucky enough to get a second bite at the cherry and sign him, but even then they weren't convinced. They kept sending him on loan to Genoa and only gave him an extended run when Nils Liedholm, scorer of Sweden's first goal in the 1958 World Cup Final, became manager.

Conti was one of the few players Enzo Bearzot brought into his Italian team after 1978; after its failure, as host, in the 1980 European Nations Cup finals, to be more exact. He was very much the modern winger, a fast, clever, energetic little player, first and foremost an outside-right but quite capable of playing on either flank. He was particularly important to the team because Franco Causio and Roberto Bettega, stars of 1978, were now past their prime. Bettega, a left-winger turned striker, like Riva, actually missed the 1982 finals with an injury. Conti hadn't the sheer, elegant class of either man, but his determination, pace and effectiveness, despite a couple of horrendous misses, first against the Cameroons in the initial round, then against Brazil in Barcelona, made no less a figure than Pelé call him the best player of 1982 tournament.

When Paolo Rossi missed an easy chance against Argentina in the previous game, it was Conti who retrieved the ball on the left-hand goal-line, returning it for Cabrini to score; Conti who flashed along the left and crossed for Rossi to head Italy's second goal in the semi-final against Poland; and Conti again who made their third goal in the Final.

That day he also far outstripped another much praised little winger, Pierre Littbarski. Young Littbarski was one of the players who had forced himself into the strong West German team after their victory in the Nations Cup. A Berliner, playing outside-right for Cologne, he was like Conti in that he was just as good on the left as on the right.

In the disgraceful 'arranged' game against Austria in Gijón, it was Littbarski who neatly put the ball on Horst Hrubesch's head from the left to score the only goal. He was also involved in both West German goals when they beat Spain 2–1 in Madrid in the opening game of the second pool. The first saw him nip in to shoot when Luis Arconada, of whom so much was fruitlessly expected, failed to hold Dremmler's long shot and, a quarter of an hour before the end, Littbarski's cross gave Klaus Fischer the second goal. In the Final, however, Italy paid him the compliment of marking him with the terrifying Gentile and, not unexpectedly perhaps, he was little seen.

Nor was the blond Karl-Heinz Rummenigge much in evidence. Hampered by a pulled thigh muscle he should not really have been playing at all, but his sudden insertion against France during extra time in Seville had brought a vital ninety-fifth minute goal, so he was reinstated despite his injury.

It is arguable that had Rummenigge been fully fit throughout, and had the powerful, dazzling Bernd Schuster been available in the midfield, Germany would have comfortably won the 1982 World Cup.

Rummenigge, who came to Bayern Munich as a very shy 19-year-old, was another natural winger, an outside-left who matured into an all-round striker. At his best he was a footballer of marvellous subtlety, elegance and finishing power, both with his foot and his head. He owed much to the intensive coaching of Dettmar Cramer, a well-travelled coach who was in charge when Rummenigge joined Bayern. Such long hours did they work together that Cramer later said they might as well have put a tent up on the ground.

It was in Argentina, where he played superbly against Mexico, once beating three opponents to score, that Rummenigge says he found true form. At first given overmuch to dribbling, the natural winger's common fault, he became a striker of great gifts, only to be sabotaged by his injury in Spain.

9 Captains and Characters

How much difference can a captain make in a World Cup? Sometimes a great deal. There is little doubt that without the inspiring example of the huge Obdulio Varela, their attacking centre-half, Uruguay would never have held out against and overcome Brazil in the deciding game of the 1950 World Cup in Rio. Despite the pressure, all the howling of the 200,000 people in the crowd, perhaps the moment which really convinced Uruguay they could win was when Varela, boldly abandoning his defensive role, steamed into the Brazilian half and hit a shot just before half-time which the keeper, Barbosa, was lucky to turn away for a corner. It may not have been quite a goal, but it happened at the very delicate moment when the teams were just about to go into the dressing rooms.

The trouble with modern football is that managers tend to be so important, so much in the public eye, that the function of skipper seems more or less limited to tossing up. This isn't always so.

When Franz Beckenbauer was West Germany's captain and sweeper in 1974, some said that he simply told Helmut Schoen, the team manager, what to do. Beckenbauer and Schoen would have laughed at this suggestion. They claimed they worked in perfect harmony and it may well be true. After all, in the World Cups of 1966 and 1970 Schoen made Beckenbauer play as a right-half and in the World Cup Final of 1966 obliged him to mark Bobby Charlton, thereby surrendering a great deal of his value to the team as an attacker. Yet on the other hand, it was Beckenbauer who, as a very young player with Bayern Munich, invented the idea of the attacking sweeper, after admiring the way Giacinto Facchetti came forward from full-back with Internazionale of Milan.

Then in 1954 there was Hungary's Ferenc Puskas. No one could deny that his influence was enormous, though not necessarily exercised for the better. He insisted on playing in the Final, though he had clearly not fully recovered from the kick on the ankle he had received from Werner Liebrich in the first match against Germany. Not only that, but his inclusion meant the exclusion of Budai who had been playing so well on the right wing, basically because Puskas didn't like him.

In the 1958 World Cup you could hardly say that Northern Ireland's Danny Blanchflower was of no account. A gifted right-half, he worked harmoniously with his clever manager, Peter Doherty, and together they devised the tactics. Blanchflower's joke was that the Irish would equalize before the other team had scored, but in fact he took a very serious approach to the game. When the crowd invaded the pitch at Windsor Park, Belfast, at the end of a 'friendly' which should (had the referee not been fog-bound) have been a World Cup match, it was Blanchflower who made every one of his players escort an Italian off the field.

Again, when his brother Jackie dropped out as centre-half after the horrifying Munich air crash that February, it was Danny who realized that tactics would have to change. There was no true successor to Jackie, no one with the same skill and versatility. Willie Cunningham, a converted full-back, did his best, but it meant that Danny, well-known for his creative play at right-half, had to play a deeper, less adventurous role to cover him.

Not all the Irish players were mesmerized by their skipper. 'Danny's a great talker!' smiled tiny, sturdy Wilbur Cush who could play wing-half, inside-forward or centre-half on demand. But there is no doubt that Danny and Doherty gave Northern Ireland their confidence and direction. Most managers are glad to have what the Italians call 'a manager on the field'.

Blanchflower, like Doherty, knew that his Northern Ireland team was a curious blend of passion and talent. It never had a decent centre-forward. It had a wonderful goalkeeper in Harry Gregg who excelled himself in the 2–2 draw against West Germany, having earlier been a hero of the Munich air crash. It had highly-gifted, constructive players in Danny himself and the inside-right, Jimmy McIlroy. But on the right wing by contrast there was Billy Bingham who, though he would later become a very able manager and take Northern Ireland honourably through to the second stage of the

1982 World Cup in Spain, was really a force of nature, an instinctive player who could not be tied down to elaborate schemes.

If Jackie Blanchflower had been fit and available the World Cup in Sweden might have been very different. As it was, injuries cut the effectiveness of the Northern Ireland team still further and, more damaging still, they were obliged to play an extra play-off game against the Czechs, who had beaten Argentina 6–1. Astonishingly they won but, exhausted and depleted, they came down with a crash in the quarter-finals against France. It had been a wonderful achievement nonetheless, a triumph of mind over matter, and would surely have been unthinkable without the captaincy of the humorous, original, irrepressible Danny Blanchflower.

In that same World Cup, David Bowen, who later became manager of Northampton Town and took them from the Fourth to the First Division, was an admirable captain for Wales. Not as elegant or talented as Blanchflower, he was one of those Welshmen who seemed to grow in stature when they put on the red shirt of their country. Originally an Arsenal player, Bowen was a great inspiration to the finely combative Welsh team which did wonderfully well to put out Hungary at Stockholm. It was a bruising play-off in which Sipos, the Hungarian stopper, was sent off for taking a wild kick at a Welsh player and Terry Medwin, the Welsh right-winger, nipped in cleverly to score from a Hungarian goal kick after a mix-up between Grosics and a defender to whom he had pushed the ball short.

In 1954 and again in 1958, West Germany not only had a forceful and dominating manager in Sepp Herberger, but an excellent captain in the strongly built Fritz Walter. He had been their unrivalled midfield general when they won the 1954 World Cup, and still looked a fine player in his veteran years when he was exposed to some distressingly rough treatment.

By contrast, it is hard to pick out an outstanding captain in Brazil's three World Cup wins. It would have seemed natural for Nilton Santos, so much the dominating figure in defence, appearing in three World Cups and rather unlucky not to play in 1950, to have skippered the 1958 and 1962 sides, but he didn't. In each case the centre-half was captain, first Bellini, then Mauro, although neither of them had Santos's authority – thirty-six years old when he won his second World Cup medal, yet still able to stroll through the Final against Czechoslovakia.

Bobby Moore was certainly of enormous importance to England in their 1966 success and in their admirable attempt to defend the Cup four years later in Mexico. This, despite his ups and downs with Alf Ramsey, not least during the England tour of the Americas in 1964. At the start of the following season, a bitter Ramsey refused to name Moore as captain for the opening game in Belfast against Northern Ireland. Indeed, he kept up the charade of appearing to consider Norman Hunter of Leeds United as an alternative for left-half until quite close to the 1966 World Cup finals. 'Pushed Bobby Moore!' he was heard to say later, with a smile.

Moore, said Ron Greenwood, who discovered, coached and launched him at West Ham United, the East London club, was 'an occasions player'. In other words, the more important the match, the more coolly and imposingly he played, whereas he was quite likely to wander through less important games and even make some curious mistakes.

He was not a natural player as he admitted himself. Tall, blond and strongly built, initially a centre-half who won a record number of England youth caps, he tended to be a little slow, was no great ball player and was not especially good in the air. But as his contemporaries at West Ham noticed from the first, he had an astonishingly cool temperament. Nothing seemed to ruffle him. West Ham turned him into a left-half, England gave him a cap in Peru on the way to the 1962 World Cup finals in Chile. He played so calmly and effectively even at the age of twenty-one that he was kept in the team for all four World Cup games and for the two World Cups after that.

In 1966 he was voted Player of the World Cup by the international journalists and how well he deserved it! True he still had faults, but he knew how to compensate for them. Thus, it was fair to say that while a quick little player operating up close to him could turn and embarrass him, Moore seldom tried to mark tight. He was essentially a great covering player with a superlative ability to read the game and a powerful tackle. Sometimes, too, his long, usually right-footed passing could set up dangerous attacks. Above all his composure, his refusal ever to worry or be harassed made him a great bulwark for his team.

Never did his serene temperament show to better advantage than in and just before the 1970 World Cup. The tournament was to be played in the breathless heights of Mexico; consequently European teams, including England, were obliged to prepare themselves at great altitude. Thus, in addition to a stay in Mexico, England also went to play in the even greater heights of Ecuador and Colombia.

There, in the seething, crime-ridden city of Bogotà, the capital of Colombia, Bobby Moore had an extraordinary and appalling experience. He, Bobby Charlton and another England player were sitting outside the so-called Green Fire jewellery shop in the Tequendama Hotel where the team was staying, when suddenly he was accused of stealing a bracelet. There was no evidence whatsoever to support this wild allegation, nor was any ever produced. Moore was allowed to leave for Quito, Ecuador, with the England team, but when they landed at Bogotà Airport on the return journey he was, amid general amazement, arrested, refused permission to fly on to Mexico City, and kept under house arrest in Bogotà.

It was soon discovered that false accusations against visiting celebrities were shamefully common in Bogotà; only a short time earlier a well-known bullfighter had apparently suffered a similar fate. After several days' detention Moore was at last allowed to join England in Guadalajara, though the charges were not dropped. Any ordinary player would have been severely affected by such a shocking experience even if they'd been playing at home in England, let alone thousands of miles away in great heat at high altitude and sometimes before hostile crowds. Not Moore: he was no ordinary player. He simply went on to play a finer World Cup than he had in 1966.

In the first match against the rough Rumanians, he played with his usually Olympian calm. Against Brazil he was simply magnificent, covering, tackling and prompting as a captain should. On retiring from the game after a spell with Fulham, including an F.A. Cup Final against his old club West Ham, he would have liked to have gone straight into management, but perhaps his very qualities of detachment, poise and quiet self-sufficiency worked against him. Of all that famous 1966 team only Jackie Charlton, solidly effective but not startlingly talented, would succeed in management. Moore, Hurst, Peters, Stiles and Ball would all try and ultimately fail.

Franz Beckenbauer played for West Germany against Moore and England in 1966 when he was a loser, and again in 1970 when his shot beneath Peter Bonetti's body in León made him a winner. In 1974, the sweeper, or '*libero*', of West Germany was at last made captain at the same time as the great Johan Cruyff was captain, centre-forward and the dominating force of Holland's brilliant team.

Time after time these two marvellous players confronted one another, sometimes when Bayern Munich met Ajax Amsterdam in the European Cup, sometimes on the international field and most notably in the 1974 World Cup Final at Munich's Olympic Stadium, when Cruyff at first seemed bound to have the best of it, but Beckenbauer prevailed in the end.

Beckenbauer was the true creator of Total Football, the basis of which was that any outfield player should be able to do anything: defenders attack, attackers defend. It never quite worked like that. As Danny Blanchflower, by then a journalist, used to say, 'I think footballers are different because people are different.' By 1974, in any case, Beckenbauer himself seemed in many ways a different, lesser player than he had been in 1972 when he played wonderfully well in Belgium to help West Germany win the Nations Cup. He was slower and far more cautious, much less ready to foray upfield from his deep position, let alone to make the kind of explosive runs so typical of him in 1972 and in 1970, when, late in the semi-final, he was cruelly chopped down on the edge of the Italian box. He hurt his shoulder so badly on that occasion that he had to play the rest of the game, the whole period of extra time, with his arm strapped to his side. Helmut Schoen's skill with substitutes, which had enabled him to win the previous game against England in León, rebounded on him: by the time Beckenbauer was injured he had used up all his substitutes. All the lurid nonsense that has been written about a great and exciting game takes no account of the truth: Italy won because they clobbered Beckenbauer.

There can be no doubt that Beckenbauer's cool presence was of immense value to West Germany in 1974, yet it is also undeniable that they looked a weary, blunt-edged team in the first round and only really came to life in the second because of the dynamic play of Rainer Bonhof, their newly selected right-half. It was Bonhof who kept them thundering forward and made the winning goal in the World Cup Final. Sprinting past Aarie Haan – Holland's emergency sweeper, moved back from midfield – on the right, he pulled the ball across for Gerd Muller to sweep past Jongbloed and score.

Total Football had one more marvellous fling in 1976, in the exhilarating finals of the Nations Cup in Yugoslavia when West Germany, with Beckenbauer again in composed command, lost the dramatic Final in Belgrade to the Czechs on penalties. Later we were to learn that it was more a matter of players than tactics.

In the early seventies West Germany suddenly found themselves with a clutch of marvellous, versatile players: Beckenbauer himself; Paul Breitner, the young attacking left-back who was so headstrong, controversial and outspoken; Uli Hoeness, splendid on the wing or in the midfield; Gerd Muller, scorer of so many memorable goals and Gunter Netzer, the long-striding inside-left.

Holland, too, had overflowed with talent. There was Cruyff, a strong-minded, sometimes wilful figure who responded to the strong management of Rinus Michels and respected him for it; Rudi Krol, the attacking full-back who became a long-lived sweeper; the tall, slow, clever, left-footed tactician Wim Van Hanegem; smoothly effective Rob Rensenbrink on the wing, and the powerful and incisive Johan Neeskens and Aarie Haan in the midfield or anywhere else they cared to play.

As time passed, however, it became clear that though a wonderful idea and one which had greatly helped to break the stranglehold of defensive play on the world game, Total Football needed too much talent and energy to be widespread.

Looking back over the history of the World Cup many mistakes have clearly been made, but somehow the competition has always had the vitality to overcome them and flourish nonetheless. That the tournament now has twenty-four finalists, with all the extra matches and fatuous stratagems (such as deciding a semi-final on penalties) this entails, is ridiculous. That it should again be played in Mexico in 1986, despite the fact that the country is bankrupt, the heights enormous and that Brazil was the obvious venue when Columbia dropped out, is scandalous.

Sometimes it almost seems as if the members of the World Cup committees have surpassed themselves in trying to devise the most curious, perverse and frustrating forms for the tournament. Nevertheless when the 1950 committee came up with the perfectly ludicrous system of a final pool decided on a league basis with no actual Final match, the tournament threw up that astonishing game between Brazil and Uruguay, the best 'Final' the World Cup has ever seen.

In 1986 another vastly elaborate scheme will produce knock-out quarter-finals, for never again can the competition run the risks of such disgracefully negative football as was seen in the second round of the 1982 tournament. The more important the World Cup becomes, the larger the sums of money at stake for winning teams and players, the greater the tendency to play safe, to close down the other side and take as few risks as possible.

Caution, you might say, is the very essence of the Italian game and was seen at its absolute worst in the first matches in Galicia. Yet in the second round, when it was essential for Italy to win against Argentina and Brazil, win they did and in the most invigorating way. Once again an absurdly devised World Cup had somehow managed to produce some marvellous football.

Yet it is still hard to forget that in 1954 there was the lunatic situation of West Germany losing 8–3 to Hungary, then going on to beat them in the Final; that in 1974 West Germany lost to East Germany in Hamburg yet still won the title, that in 1978 Argentina qualified on goal difference (itself an absurdity) in the most dubious way, at the expense of an outraged Brazil.

Planning a World Cup is an impossible task. The attempt to reconcile the basic knock-out, sudden-death idea of a cup competition with the 'fairness' of a league tournament is doomed from the start.

João Havelange's spell as President of FIFA has been an uneasy time for the game and the World Cup. He brought in the twenty-four-team finals as a sop to the Afro-Asian countries who voted him into office; then violently opposed, for apparently quite personal reasons, the playing of the 1986 World Cup in Brazil. He and the President of the Brazilian Confederation of Football, Coutinho, were at daggers drawn on the issue.

The disappointing truth, as far as the Afro-Asian countries are concerned, is that they have made little contribution to the World Cup. Ideally, the qualifying tournaments should be de-zoned, rather than played on a narrowly geographical basis. This would allow countries to qualify on merit rather than because they happen to come from a certain continent or hemisphere. No one can deny the contribution made by the gallant little North Koreans to the 1966 World Cup or the excellence of Algeria's 1982 displays against West Germany and Chile, but the North Koreans sank without trace and, strangely, African football has failed to express the bubbling talents of its individual players.

Many African players, however, have found fame in Europe. In 1966 the powerful Portuguese World Cup team's greatest star was the Mozambiquan Eusebio, and its excellent captain, the muscular left-half, Mario Coluna, with his stunning shot and clever technique. Out of Africa, always something new, said the Romans. In football the something new tends to be a player, rather than a consistent team. Organization is lacking.

Perhaps it is too much to hope for an improvement in refereeing. In the 1978 and 1982 World Cups it was almost uniformly appalling, so that by the end a kind of anarchy seemed to prevail. The 1978 World Cup Final between Holland and Argentina was an absolute disgrace in sporting terms. In the 1982 Final, Bruno Conti committed Italy's first foul of a deplorable first half in the opening minute; similarly, in the opening minute of the 1978 Final, the Dutch committed the first foul of a match which was to be marred by over fifty fouls. Any neutral observer would agree that Gonella, the limp Italian referee, indulged Argentina, as had so many referees, in the 1978 game.

Four years later Brazil's Coelho had little control over the Italians and West Germans. Shortly before half-time, Oriali, the Italian midfield player, was racing through for goal when Uli Stielike, the West German sweeper, quite callously blocked him. Coelho didn't even take Stielike's name, but merely gave a free-kick outside the penalty area. However, under the sensible new rule applied in the English League the following season, such 'professional fouls' were punished by expulsion.

Clever players must be protected or football dies. Oddly enough, the Brazilians and Argentines, who over the decades have produced so many marvellous ball players, have always been pretty ruthless as well, though in this respect the Argentines have a far worse record than Brazil.

Brazil, indeed, has surely contributed more to the World Cup than any other country. Their debut in 1930 was unimpressive, even though they were playing on South American soil, but at that time black players had yet to make their full impact on Brazilian football.

For years they were discouraged. Many leading clubs would not have them in their team. But once black players began to be chosen, the Brazilian game changed in the most dramatic and spectacular way. With their agility, superlative control, and superb reflexes untouched by formal training, black players began to introduce inventive, original techniques never seen before.

Brazil went out to Italy in the first round in 1934, but by 1938 they had a magnificent side which would surely have knocked out Italy in the semi-final in France, were it not for the folly of leaving out the two attacking stars, Leonidas and Tim.

In 1950, though they lost the deciding match to Uruguay, the Brazilians played a style of football against Spain and Sweden the likes of which had never been seen before, unrivalled for sheer excitement, skill, speed and swift combination. In 1954 they disgraced themselves in the Battle of Berne, as they had in the Battle of Bordeaux in 1938, yet when they wanted to play they were still a fine, attractive team.

In 1958 they at last got it right with their four-in-a-line defence and astounded the world with Pelé, Garrincha and their master spirit Didì in midfield. In 1962 they won again, though a little less impressively, but in 1970 their team was a joy to watch and how well they deserved to be handed the World Cup for keeps, after their third triumph.

In 1982, though Italy ambushed them and they no longer had their old stars in attack, they still played the finest football of the tournament, leaving those lucky enough to have seen them with the most golden memories of that uneven and often disappointingly negative World Cup.

Italy, too, have won the Cup three times, but in sharp contrast with Brazil, few outside Italy itself applauded their laborious, sometimes ruthless success of 1934, though in 1938 they did play much fluent football. As for 1982, there can be no doubt that they did wonderfully well to knock out such strong teams as Argentina and Brazil. They were far too good for Poland in the semi-finals and after their 'pact' with Austria and the excesses of Harald Schumacher, for West Germany to have won the Final would have been an insult to the game.

Brazil may have hiccoughed badly in 1966, been found wanting in 1978, but all in all, they and their great players, from Leonidas to Pelé and Garrincha, from Didì to Gerson and Rivelino, from Julinho to Jairzinho, from Zito to Zico and the Santoses to Falcão, have been the lifeblood of this great competition.

The tournament's aim has always been to present the best of football in the best of circumstances. Even if it has sometimes made it wilfully difficult, who can deny that the World Cup is still vibrantly alive?

World Cup Results 1930–82

Uruguay 1930

Pool I

France 4, Mexico 1 (HT 3–0)
Argentina 1, France 0 (HT 0–0)
Chile 3, Mexico 0 (HT 1–0)
Chile 1, France 0 (HT 0–0)
Argentina 6, Mexico 3 (HT 3–0)
Argentina 3, Chile 1 (HT 2–1)

					GOALS		
	P	W	D	L	F	A	PTS
Argentina	3	3	0	0	10	4	6
Chile	3	2	0	1	5	3	4
France	3	1	0	2	4	3	2
Mexico	3	0	0	3	4	13	0

Pool II

Yugoslavia 2, Brazil 1 (HT 2–0)
Yugoslavia 4, Bolivia 0 (HT 0–0)
Brazil 4, Bolivia 0 (HT 1–0)

					GOALS		
	P	W	D	L	F	A	PTS
Yugoslavia	2	2	0	0	6	1	4
Brazil	2	1	0	1	5	2	2
Bolivia	2	0	0	2	0	8	0

Pool III

Romania 3, Peru 1 (HT 1–0)
Uruguay 1, Peru 0 (HT 0–0)
Uruguay 4, Romania 0 (HT 4–0)

					GOALS		
	P	W	D	L	F	A	PTS
Uruguay	2	2	0	0	5	0	4
Romania	2	1	0	1	3	5	2
Peru	2	0	0	2	1	4	0

Pool IV

United States 3, Belgium 0 (HT 2–0)
United States 3, Paraguay 0 (HT 2–0)
Paraguay 1, Belgium 0 (HT 1–0)

					GOALS		
	P	W	D	L	F	A	PTS
United States	2	2	0	0	6	0	4
Paraguay	2	1	0	1	1	3	2
Belgium	2	0	0	2	0	4	0

Semi-finals

Argentina 6
Botasso; Della Torre, Paternoster; Evaristo, J., Monti, Orlandini; Peucelle, Scopelli, Stabile, Ferreira (capt.), Evaristo, M.

United States 1
Douglas; Wood, Moorhouse; Gallacher, Tracey, Auld; Brown, Gonsalvez, Patenaude, Florie (capt.), McGhee.

SCORERS
Monti, Scopelli, Stabile (2), Peucelle (2), for Argentina

Brown for United States

(HT 1–0)

Uruguay 6
Ballesteros; Nasazzi (capt.), Mascheroni; Andrade, Fernandez, Gestido; Dorado, Scarone, Anselmo, Cea, Iriarte.

Yugoslavia 1
Yavocic; Ivkovic (capt.), Milhailovic; Arsenievic, Stefanovic, Djokic; Tirnanic, Marianovic, Beck, Vujadinovic, Seculic.

SCORERS

Cea (3), Anselmo (2), Iriarte for Uruguay

Seculic for Yugoslavia

(HT 3–1)

Final

Uruguay 4
Ballesteros; Nasazzi (capt.), Mascheroni; Andrade, Fernandez, Gestido; Dorado, Scarone, Castro, Cea, Iriarte.

Argentina 2
Botasso; Della Torre, Paternoster; Evaristo, J., Monti, Suarez; Peucelle, Varallo, Stabile, Ferreira (capt'.), Evaristo, M

SCORERS

Dorado, Cea, Iriarte, Castro for Uruguay

Peucelle, Stabile for Argentina

(HT 1–2)

Italy 1934

First round

Italy 7, United States 1 (HT 3–0)
Czechoslovakia 2, Romania 1 (HT 0–1)
Germany 5, Belgium 2 (HT 1–2)
Austria 3, France 2 (HT 1–1, 1–1) after extra time
Spain 3, Brazil 1 (HT 3–1)
Switzerland 3, Holland 2 (HT 2–1)
Sweden 3, Argentina 2 (HT 1–1)
Hungary 4, Egypt 2 (HT 2–1)

Second round

Germany 2, Sweden 1 (HT 1–0)
Austria 2, Hungary 1 (HT 1–0)
Italy 1, Spain 1 (HT 1–0, 1–1) after extra time
Italy 1, Spain 0 (HT 1–0) replay
Czechoslovakia 3, Switzerland 2 (HT 1–1)

Semi-finals

Rome

Czechoslovakia 3
Planicka (capt.); Burger, Ctyroky; Kostalek, Cambal, Krcil; Junek, Svoboda, Sobotka, Nejedly, Puc.

Germany 1
Kress; Haringer, Busch; Zielinski, Szepan (capt.), Bender; Lehner, Siffling, Conen, Noack, Kobierski.

SCORERS
Nejedly (2), Krcil for Czechoslovakia

Noack for Germany

(HT 1–0)

Milan

Italy 1	Austria 0
Combi (capt.); Monzeglio, Allemandi; Ferraris IV, Monti, Bertolini; Guaita, Meazza, Schiavio, Ferrari, Orsi.	Platzer; Cisar, Seszta; Wagner, Smistik (capt.), Urbanek; Zischek, Bican, Sindelar, Schall, Viertel.

SCORER
Guaita for Italy
(HT 1–0)

Third place match

Naples

Germany 3	Austria 2
Jakob; Janes, Busch; Zielinski, Muenzenberg, Bender; Lehner, Siffling, Conen, Szepan (capt.), Heidemann.	Platzer; Cisar, Seszta, Wagner, Smistik (capt.), Urbanek; Zischek, Braun, Bican, Horwath, Viertel.

SCORERS

Lehner (2), Conen for Germany	Seszta for Austria

(HT 3–1)

Final

Rome

Italy 2 (after extra time)	Czechoslovakia 1
Combi (capt.); Monzeglio, Allemandi; Ferraris IV, Monti, Bertolini; Guaita, Meazza, Schiavio, Ferrari, Orsi.	Planicka (capt.); Zenisek, Ctyroky; Kostalek, Cambal, Krcil; Junek, Svoboda, Sobotka, Nejedly, Puc.

SCORERS

Orsi, Schiavio for Italy	Puc for Czechoslovakia

(HT 0–0)

France 1938

First round

Switzerland 1, Germany 1 (HT 1–1, 1–1) after extra time
Switzerland 4, Germany 2 (HT 0–2) replay
Cuba 3, Romania 3 (HT 0–1, 3–3) after extra time
Cuba 2, Romania 1 (HT 0–1) replay
Hungary 6, Dutch East Indies 0 (HT 4–0)
France 3, Belgium 1 (HT 2–1)
Czechoslovakia 3, Holland 0 (HT 0–0, 0–0) after extra time
Brazil 6, Poland 5 (HT 3–1, 4–4) after extra time
Italy 2, Norway 1 (HT 1–0, 1–1) after extra time

Second round

Sweden 8, Cuba 0 (HT 4–0)
Hungary 2, Switzerland 0 (HT 1–0)
Italy 3, France 1 (HT 1–1)
Brazil 1, Czechoslovakia 1 (HT 1–1, 1–1) after extra time
Brazil 2, Czechoslovakia 1 (HT 0–1) replay

Semi-finals

Marseilles

Italy 2
Olivieri; Foni, Rava; Serantoni, Andreolo, Locatelli; Biavati, Meazza (capt.), Piola, Ferrari, Colaussi.

Brazil 1
Walter; Domingas Da Guia, Machados; Zeze, Martin (capt.), Alfonsinho; Lopez, Luisinho, Peracio, Romeo, Patesko.

SCORERS
Colaussi, Meazza (penalty) for Italy
Romeo for Brazil
(HT 2–0)

Paris

Hungary 5
Szabo; Koranyi, Biro; Szalay, Turai, Lazar; Sas, Szengeller, Sarosi (capt.), Toldi, Titkos.

Sweden 1
Abrahamson; Eriksson, Kjellgren; Almgren, Jacobsson, Svanstroem, Wetterstroem, Keller (capt.), Andersson, H., Jonasson, Nyberg.

SCORERS
Szengeller (3), Titkos, Sarosi for Hungary

Nyberg for Sweden

(HT 3–1)

Third place match

Bordeaux

Brazil 4
Batatoes; Domingas Da Guia, Machados; Zeze, Brandao, Alfonsinho; Roberto, Romeo, Leonidas (capt.), Peracio, Patesko.

Sweden 2
Abrahamson; Eriksson, Nilssen; Almgren, Linderholm, Svanstroem (capt.), Berssen, Andersson, H., Jonasson, Andersson, A., Nyberg.

SCORERS
Romeo, Leonidas (2), Peracio for Brazil

Jonasson, Nyberg for Sweden

(HT 1–2)

Final

Paris

Italy 4
Olivieri; Foni, Rava, Serantoni, Andreolo, Locatelli; Biavati, Meazza (capt.), Piola, Ferrari, Colaussi.

Hungary 2
Szabo; Polgar, Biro; Szalay, Szucs, Lazar; Sas, Vincze, Sarosi (capt.), Szengeller, Titkos.

SCORERS
Colaussi (2), Piola (2) for Italy

Titkos, Sarosi for Hungary

(HT 3–1)

Brazil 1950

Pool I

Brazil 4, Mexico 0 (HT 1–0)
Yugoslavia 3, Switzerland 0 (HT 3–0)
Yugoslavia 4, Mexico 1 (HT 2–0)
Brazil 2, Switzerland 2 (HT 2–1)
Brazil 2, Yugoslavia 0 (HT 1–0)
Switzerland 2, Mexico 1 (HT 2–0)

					GOALS		
	P	W	D	L	F	A	PTS
Brazil	3	2	1	0	8	2	5
Yugoslavia	3	2	0	1	7	3	4
Switzerland	3	1	1	1	4	6	3
Mexico	3	0	0	3	2	10	0

Pool II

Spain 3, United States 1 (HT 0–1)
England 2, Chile 0 (HT 1–0)
United States 1, England 0 (HT 1–0)
Spain 2, Chile 0 (HT 2–0)
Spain 1, England 0 (HT 0–0)
Chile 5, United States 2 (HT 2–0)

					GOALS		
	P	W	D	L	F	A	PTS
Spain	3	3	0	0	6	1	6
England	3	1	0	2	2	2	2
Chile	3	1	0	2	5	6	2
United States	3	1	0	2	4	8	2

Pool III

Sweden 3, Italy 2 (HT 2–1)
Sweden 2, Paraguay 2 (HT 2–1)
Italy 2, Paraguay 0 (HT 1–0)

					GOALS		
	P	W	D	L	F	A	PTS
Sweden	2	1	1	0	5	4	3
Italy	2	1	0	1	4	3	2
Paraguay	2	0	1	1	2	4	1

Pool IV

Uruguay 8, Bolivia 0 (HT 4–0)

					GOALS		
	P	W	D	L	F	A	PTS
Uruguay	1	1	0	0	8	0	2
Bolivia	1	0	0	1	0	8	0

Final pool matches

São Paulo

Uruguay 2
Maspoli; Gonzales, M., Tejera; Gonzales, W., Varela (capt.), Andrade; Ghiggia, Perez, Miguez, Schiaffino, Vidal.

Spain 2
Ramallets; Alonzo, Gonzalvo II; Gonzalvo III, Parra, Puchades; Basora, Igoa, Zarra, Molowny, Gainza.

SCORERS
Ghiggia, Varela for Uruguay
Basora (2) for Spain
(HT 1–2)

Rio

Brazil 7
Barbosa; Augusto (capt.), Juvenal; Bauer, Danilo, Bigode; Maneca, Zizinho, Ademir, Jair, Chico.

Sweden 1
Svensson; Samuelsson, Nilsson, E.; Andersson, Nordahl, K., Gard; Sundqvist, Palmer, Jeppson, Skoglund, Nilsson, S.

SCORERS
Ademir (4), Chico (2), Maneca for Brazil
Andersson (penalty) for Sweden
(HT 3–0)

São Paulo

Uruguay 3
Paz; Gonzales, M., Tejera; Gambetta, Varela (capt.), Andrade; Ghiggia, Perez, Miguez, Schiaffino, Vidal.

Sweden 2
Svensson; Samuelsson, Nilsson, E.; Andersson, Johansson, Gard, Johnsson, Palmer, Mellberg, Skoglund, Sundqvist.

SCORERS
Ghiggia, Miguez (2) for Uruguay
Palmer, Sundqvist for Sweden
(HT 1–2)

Rio

Brazil 6
Barbosa; Augusto (capt.), Juvenal; Bauer, Danilo, Bigode; Friaça, Zizinho, Ademir, Jair, Chico.

Spain 1
Eizaguirre; Alonzo, Gonzalvo II; Gonzalvo III, Parra, Puchades; Basora, Igoa, Zarra, Panizo, Gainza.

SCORERS
Jair (2), Chico (2), Zizinho, Parra (own goal) for Brazil
Igoa for Spain
(HT 3–0)

São Paulo

Sweden 3
Svensson; Samuelsson, Nilsson, E., Andersson, Johansson, Gard; Sundqvist, Mellberg, Rydell, Palmer, Johnsson.

Spain 1
Eizaguirre; Asensi, Alonzo; Silva, Parra, Puchades; Basora, Fernandez, Zarra, Panizo, Juncosa.

SCORERS
Johansson, Mellberg, Palmer for Sweden
Zarra for Spain
(HT 2–0)

Rio

Uruguay 2
Maspoli; Gonzales, M., Tejera; Gambetta, Varela (capt.), Andrade; Ghiggia, Perez, Miguez, Schiaffino, Moran.

Brazil 1
Barbosa; Augusto (capt.), Juvenal; Bauer, Danilo, Bigode; Friaça, Zizinho, Ademir, Jair, Chico.

SCORERS
Schiaffino, Ghiggia for Uruguay
Friaça for Brazil
(HT 0–0)

Final positions

					GOALS		
	P	W	D	L	F	A	PTS
Uruguay	3	2	1	0	7	5	5
Brazil	3	2	0	1	14	4	4
Sweden	3	1	0	2	6	11	2
Spain	3	0	1	2	4	11	1

Switzerland 1954

Pool I

Yugoslavia 1, France 0 (HT 1–0)
Brazil 5, Mexico 0 (HT 4–0)
France 3, Mexico 2 (HT 1–0)
Brazil 1, Yugoslavia 1 (HT 0–1) after extra time

					GOALS		
	P	W	D	L	F	A	PTS
Brazil	2	1	1	0	6	1	3
Yugoslavia	2	1	1	0	2	1	3
France	2	1	0	1	3	3	2
Mexico	2	0	0	2	2	8	0

Pool II

Hungary 9, Korea 0 (HT 4–0)
West Germany 4, Turkey 1 (HT 1–1)
Hungary 8, West Germany 3 (HT 3–1)
Turkey 7, Korea 0 (HT 4–0)

					GOALS		
	P	W	D	L	F	A	PTS
Hungary	2	2	0	0	17	3	4
West Germany	2	1	0	1	7	9	2
Turkey	2	1	0	1	8	4	2
Korea	2	0	0	2	0	16	0

Play off West Germany 7, Turkey 2 (HT 3–1)

Pool III

Austria 1, Scotland 0 (HT 1–0)
Uruguay 2, Czechoslovakia 0 (HT 0–0)
Austria 5, Czechoslovakia 0 (HT 4–0)
Uruguay 7, Scotland 0 (HT 2–0)

					GOALS		
	P	W	D	L	F	A	PTS
Uruguay	2	2	0	0	9	0	4
Austria	2	2	0	0	6	0	4
Czechoslovakia	2	0	0	2	0	7	0
Scotland	2	0	0	2	0	8	0

Pool IV

England 4, Belgium 4 (HT 2–1)
England 2, Switzerland 0 (HT 1–0)
Switzerland 2, Italy 1 (HT 1–1)
Italy 4, Belgium 1 (HT 1–0)

					GOALS		
	P	W	D	L	F	A	PTS
England	2	1	1	0	6	4	3
Italy	2	1	0	1	5	3	2
Switzerland	2	1	0	1	2	3	2
Belgium	2	0	1	1	5	8	1

Play off Switzerland 4, Italy 1 (HT 1–0)

Quarter-finals

Geneva

West Germany 2
Turek; Laband, Kohlmeyer; Eckel, Liebrich, Mai; Rahn, Morlock, Walter, O., Walter, F. (capt.), Schaefer.

Yugoslavia 0
Beara; Stankovic, Crnkovic; Cjaicowski, I., Horvat, Boskov; Milutinovic, Mitic (capt.), Vukas, Bobek, Zebec.

SCORERS
Horvat (own goal), Rahn for West Germany
(HT 1–0)

Berne

Hungary 4
Grosics; Buzansky, Lantos; Bozsik (capt.), Lorant, Zakarias; Toth, M., Kocsis, Hidegkuti, Czibor, Toth, J.

Brazil 2
Castilho; Santos, D., Santos, N.; Brandaozinho, Pinheiro (capt.), Bauer; Julinho, Didì, Indio, Tozzi, Maurinho.

SCORERS
Hidegkuti (2), Kocsis, Lantos (penalty) for Hungary

Santos, D. (penalty), Julinho for Brazil

(HT 2–1)

Lausanne

Austria 7
Schmied; Hanappi, Barschandt; Ocwirk (capt.), Happel, Koller; Koerner, R., Wagner, Stojaspal, Probst, Koerner, A.

Switzerland 5
Parlier; Neury, Kernen; Eggimann, Bocquet (capt.), Casali; Antenen, Vonlanthen, Hugi, Ballaman, Fatton.

SCORERS
Koerner, A. (2), Ocwirk, Wagner (3), Probst for Austria

Ballaman (2), Hugi (2), Hanappi (own goal) for Switzerland

(HT 2–4)

Basel

Uruguay 4
Maspoli; Santamaria, Martinez; Andrade, Varela (capt.), Cruz; Abbadie, Ambrois, Miguez, Schiaffino, Borges.

England 2
Merrick; Staniforth, Byrne; McGarry, Wright (capt.), Dickinson; Matthews, Broadis, Lofthouse, Wilshaw, Finney.

SCORERS
Borges, Varela, Schiaffino, Ambrois for Uruguay

Lofthouse, Finney for England

(HT 2–1)

Semi-finals

Basel

West Germany 6	Austria 1
Turek; Posipal, Kohlmeyer; Eckel, Liebrich, Mai; Rahn, Morlock, Walter, O., Walter, F. (capt.), Schaefer.	Zeman; Hanappi, Schleger; Ocwirk (capt.), Happel, Koller; Koerner, R., Wagner, Stojaspal, Probst, Koerner, A.
SCORERS	
Schaefer, Morlock, Walter, F. (2 penalties), Walter, O. (2) for West Germany	Probst for Austria
(HT 1–0)	

Lausanne

Hungary 4 (after extra time)	Uruguay 2
Grosics; Buzansky, Lantos; Boszik (capt.), Lorant, Zakarias; Budai, Kocsis, Palotas, Hidegkuti, Czibor.	Maspoli; Santamaria, Martinez; Andrade (capt.), Carballo, Cruz; Souto, Ambrois, Schiaffino, Hohberg, Borges.
SCORERS	
Czibor, Hidegkuti, Kocsis (2) for Hungary	Hohberg (2) for Uruguay
(HT 1–0)	

Third place match

Zurich

Austria 3	Uruguay 1
Schmied; Hanappi, Barschandt; Ocwirk (capt.), Kollmann, Koller; Koerner, R., Wagner, Dienst, Stojaspal, Probst.	Maspoli; Santamaria, Martinez; Andrade (capt.), Carballo, Cruz; Abbadie, Hohberg, Mendez, Schiaffino, Borges.
SCORERS	
Stojaspal (penalty), Cruz (own goal), Ocwirk for Austria	Hohberg for Uruguay
(HT 1–1)	

Final

Berne

West Germany 3
Turek; Posipal, Kohlmeyer; Eckel, Liebrich, Mai; Rahn, Morlock, Walter, O., Walter, F., Schaefer.

Hungary 2
Grosics; Buzansky, Lantos; Bozsik, Lorant, Zakarias; Czibor, Kocsis, Hidegkuti, Puskas, Toth, J.

SCORERS
Morlock, Rahn (2) for West Germany

Puskas, Czibor for Hungary

(HT 2–2)

Sweden 1958

Pool I

West Germany 3, Argentina 1 (HT 2–1)
Ireland 1, Czechoslovakia 0 (HT 1–0)
West Germany 2, Czechoslovakia 2 (HT 1–0)
Argentina 3, Ireland 1 (HT 1–1)
West Germany 2, Ireland 2 (HT 1–1)
Czechoslovakia 6, Argentina 1 (HT 3–1)

					GOALS		
	P	W	D	L	F	A	PTS
West Germany	3	1	2	0	7	5	4
Czechoslovakia	3	1	1	1	8	4	3
Ireland	3	1	1	1	4	5	3
Argentina	3	1	0	2	5	10	2

Pool II

France 7, Paraguay 3 (HT 2–2)
Yugoslavia 1, Scotland 1 (HT 1–0)
Yugoslavia 3, France 2 (HT 1–1)
Paraguay 3, Scotland 2 (HT 2–1)
France 2, Scotland 1 (HT 2–0)
Yugoslavia 3, Paraguay 3 (HT 2–1)

					GOALS		
	P	W	D	L	F	A	PTS
France	3	2	0	1	11	7	4
Yugoslavia	3	1	2	0	7	6	4
Paraguay	3	1	1	1	9	12	3
Scotland	3	0	1	2	4	6	1

Pool III

Sweden 3, Mexico 0 (HT 1–0)
Hungary 1, Wales 1 (HT 1–1)
Wales 1, Mexico 1 (HT 1–1)
Sweden 2, Hungary 1 (HT 1–0)
Sweden 0, Wales 0 (HT 0–0)
Hungary 4, Mexico 0 (HT 1–0)

					GOALS		
	P	W	D	L	F	A	PTS
Sweden	3	2	1	0	5	1	5
Hungary	3	1	1	1	6	3	3
Wales	3	0	3	0	2	2	3
Mexico	3	0	1	2	1	8	1

Play off Wales 2, Hungary 1 (HT 0–1)

Pool IV

England 2, Russia 2 (HT 0–1)
Brazil 3, Austria 0 (HT 1–0)
England 0, Brazil 0 (HT 0–0)
Russia 2, Austria 0 (HT 1–0)
Brazil 2, Russia 0 (HT 1–0)
England 2, Austria 2 (HT 0–1)

					GOALS		
	P	W	D	L	F	A	PTS
Brazil	3	2	1	0	5	0	5
England	3	0	3	0	4	4	3
Russia	3	1	1	1	4	4	3
Austria	3	0	1	2	2	7	1

Play off Russia 1, England 0 (HT 0–0)

Quarter-finals

Norrköping

France 4
Abbes; Kaelbel, Lerond; Penverne, Jonquet, Marcel; Wisnieski, Fontaine, Kopa, Piantoni, Vincent.

Ireland 0
Gregg; Keith, McMichael; Blanchflower, Cunningham, Cush; Bingham, Casey, Scott, McIlroy, McParland.

SCORERS
Wisnieski, Fontaine (2), Piantoni for France
(HT 1–0)

Malmö

West Germany 1
Herkenrath; Stollenwerk, Juskowiak; Eckel, Erhardt, Szymaniak; Rahn, Walter, Seeler, Schmidt, Schaefer.

Yugoslavia 0
Krivocuka; Sijakovic, Crnkovic; Krstic, Zebec, Boskov; Petakovic, Veselinovic, Milutinovic, Ognjanovic, Rajkov.

SCORER
Rahn for West Germany
(HT 1–0)

Stockholm

Sweden 2
Svensson; Bergmark, Axbom; Boerjesson, Gustavsson, Parling; Hamrin, Gren, Simonsson, Liedholm, Skoglund.

Russia 0
Yachine; Kessarev, Kuznetsov; Voinov, Krijevski, Tsarev; Ivanov, A., Ivanov, V., Simonian, Salnikov, Ilyin.

SCORERS
Hamrin, Simonsson for Sweden
(HT 0–0)

Gothenburg

Brazil 1
Gilmar; De Sordi, Santos, N.; Zito, Bellini, Orlando; Garrincha, Didì, Mazzola, Pelé, Zagalo.

Wales 0
Kelsey; Williams, Hopkins; Sullivan, Charles, M., Bowen; Medwin, Hewitt, Webster, Allchurch, Jones.

SCORER
Pelé for Brazil
(HT 0–0)

Semi-finals

Stockholm

Brazil 5
Gilmar; De Sordi, Santos, N.; Zito, Bellini, Orlando; Garrincha, Didì, Vavà, Pelé, Zagalo.

France 2
Abbes; Kaelbel, Lerond; Penverne, Jonquet, Marcel; Wisnieski, Fontaine, Kopa, Piantoni, Vincent.

SCORERS
Vavà, Didì, Pelé (3) for Brazil
Fontaine, Piantoni for France
(HT 2–1)

Gothenburg

Sweden 3
Svensson; Bergmark, Axbom; Boerjesson, Gustavsson, Parling; Hamrin, Gren, Simonsson, Liedholm, Skoglund.

West Germany 1
Herkenrath; Stollenwerk, Juskowiak; Eckel, Erhardt, Szymaniak; Rahn, Walter, Seeler, Schaefer, Cieslarczyk.

SCORERS
Skoglund, Gren, Hamrin for Sweden
Schaefer for West Germany
(HT 1–1)

Third place match

Gothenburg

France 6
Abbes; Kaelbel, Lerond; Penverne, Lafont, Marcel; Wisnieski, Douis, Kopa, Fontaine, Vincent.

West Germany 3
Kwiatowski; Stollenwerk, Erhardt; Schnellinger, Wewers, Szymaniak; Rahn, Sturm, Kelbassa, Schaefer, Cieslarczyk.

SCORERS
Fontaine (4), Kopa (penalty), Douis for France
Cieslarezyk, Rahn, Schaefer for West Germany
(HT 3–1)

Final

Stockholm

Brazil 5
Gilmar; Santos, D., Santos, N.; Zito, Bellini, Orlando; Garrincha, Didì, Vavà, Pelé, Zagalo.

Sweden 2
Svensson; Bergmark, Axbom, Boerjesson, Gustavsson, Parling. Hamrin, Gren, Simonsson, Liedholm, Skoglund

SCORERS
Vavà (2), Pelé (2), Zagalo for Brazil
Liedholm, Simonsson for Sweden
(HT 2–1)

Chile 1962

Group I

Uruguay 2, Colombia 1 (HT 0–1)
Russia 2, Yugoslavia 0 (HT 0–0)
Yugoslavia 3, Uruguay 1 (HT 2–1)
Russia 4, Colombia 4 (HT 3–1)
Russia 2, Uruguay 1 (HT 1–0)
Yugoslavia 5, Colombia 0 (HT 2–0)

					GOALS		
	P	W	D	L	F	A	PTS
Russia	3	2	1	0	8	5	5
Yugoslavia	3	2	0	1	8	3	4
Uruguay	3	1	0	2	4	6	2
Colombia	3	0	1	2	5	11	1

Group II

Chile 3, Switzerland 1 (HT 1–1)
West Germany 0, Italy 0 (HT 0–0)
Chile 2, Italy 0 (HT 0–0)
West Germany 2, Switzerland 1 (HT 1–0)
West Germany 2, Chile 0 (HT 1–0)
Italy 3, Switzerland 0 (HT 1–0)

					GOALS		
	P	W	D	L	F	A	PTS
West Germany	3	2	1	0	4	1	5
Chile	3	2	0	1	5	3	4
Italy	3	1	1	1	3	2	3
Switzerland	3	0	0	3	2	8	0

Group III

Brazil 2, Mexico 0 (HT 0–0)
Czechoslovakia 1, Spain 0 (HT 0–0)
Brazil 0, Czechoslovakia 0 (HT 0–0)
Spain 1, Mexico 0 (HT 0–0)
Brazil 2, Spain 1 (HT 0–1)
Mexico 3, Czechoslovakia 1 (HT 2–1)

					GOALS		
	P	W	D	L	F	A	PTS
Brazil	3	2	1	0	4	1	5
Czechoslovakia	3	1	1	1	2	3	3
Mexico	3	1	0	2	3	4	2
Spain	3	1	0	2	2	3	2

Group IV

Argentina 1, Bulgaria 0 (HT 1–0)
Hungary 2, England 1 (HT 1–0)
England 3, Argentina 1 (HT 2–0)
Hungary 6, Bulgaria 1 (HT 4–0)
Argentina 0, Hungary 0 (HT 0–0)
England 0, Bulgaria 0 (HT 0–0)

					GOALS		
	P	W	D	L	F	A	PTS
Hungary	3	2	1	0	8	2	5
England	3	1	1	1	4	3	3
Argentina	3	1	1	1	2	3	3
Bulgaria	3	0	1	2	1	7	1

Quarter-finals

Santiago

Yugoslavia 1
Soskic; Durkovic, Jusufi; Radakovic, Markovic, Popovic; Kovacevic, Sekularac, Jerkovic, Galic, Skoblar.

West Germany 0
Fahrian; Novak, Schnellinger; Schulz, Erhardt, Giesemann; Haller, Szymaniak, Seeler, Brulls, Schaefer.

SCORER
Radakovic for Yugoslavia
(HT 0–0)

Viña del Mar

Brazil 3
Gilmar; Santos, D., Mauro, Zozimo, Santos, N.; Zito, Didì, Garrincha, Vavà, Amarildo, Zagalo.

England 1
Springett; Armfield, Wilson; Moore, Norman, Flowers; Douglas, Greaves, Hitchens, Haynes, Charlton.

SCORERS
Garrincha (2), Vavà for Brazil
Hitchens for England
(HT 1–1)

Arico

Chile 2
Escutti; Eyzaguirre, Contreras, Sanchez, R., Navarro; Toro, Rojas; Ramirez, Landa, Tobar, Sanchez, L.

Russia 1
Yachine; Tchokelli, Ostrovski; Voronin, Maslenkin, Netto; Chislenko, Ivanov, Ponedelnik, Mamikin, Meshki.

SCORERS
Sanchez, L., Rojas for Chile
Chislenko for Russia
(HT 2–1)

Rancagua

Czechoslovakia 1
Schroiff; Lala, Novak; Pluskal, Popluhar, Masopust; Pospichal, Scherer, Kvasniak, Kadraba, Jelinek.

Hungary 0
Grosics; Matrai, Sarosi; Solymosi, Meszoly, Sipos; Sandor, Rakosi, Albert, Tichy, Fenyvesi.

SCORER
Scherer for Czechoslovakia
(HT 1–0)

Semi-finals

Santiago

Brazil 4
Gilmar; Santos, D., Mauro, Zozimo, Santos, N.; Zito, Didì, Garrincha, Vavà, Amarildo, Zagalo.

Chile 2
Escutti; Eyzaguirre, Contreras, Sanchez, R., Rodriguez; Toro, Rojas; Ramirez, Landa, Tobar, Sanchez, L.

SCORERS
Garrincha (2), Vavà (2) for Brazil

Toro, Sanchez, L. (penalty) for Chile

(HT 2–1)

Viña del Mar

Czechoslovakia 3
Schroiff; Lala, Novak; Pluskal, Popluhar, Masopust; Pospichal, Scherer, Kvasniak, Kadraba, Jelinek.

Yugoslavia 1
Soskic; Durkovic, Jusufi; Radakovic, Markovic, Popovic; Sujakovic, Sekularac, Jerkovic, Galic, Skoblar.

SCORERS
Kadraba, Scherer (2) for Czechoslovakia

Jerkovic for Yugoslavia

(HT 0–0)

Third place match

Santiago

Chile 1
Godoy; Eyzaguirre, Cruz, Sanchez, R., Rodriguez; Toro, Rojas; Ramirez, Campos, Tobar, Sanchez, L.

Yugoslavia 0
Soskic; Durkovic, Svinjarevic; Radakovic, Markovic, Popovic; Kovacevic, Sekularac, Jerkovic, Galic, Skoblar.

SCORER
Rojas for Chile
(HT 0–0)

Final

Santiago

Brazil 3	Czechoslovakia 1
Gilmar; Santos, D., Mauro, Zozimo, Santos, N.; Zito, Didì, Garrincha, Vavà, Amarildo, Zagalo.	Schroiff; Tichy, Novak; Pluskal, Popluhar, Masopust; Pospichal, Scherer, Kvasniak, Kadraba, Jelinek.

SCORERS

Amarildo, Zito, Vavà for Brazil	Masopust for Czechoslovakia

(HT 1–1)

England 1966

Group I

England 0, Uruguay 0 (HT 0–0)
France 1, Mexico 1 (HT 0–0)
Uruguay 2, France 1 (HT 2–1)
England 2, Mexico 0 (HT 1–0)
Uruguay 0, Mexico 0 (HT 0–0)
England 2, France 0 (HT 1–0)

					GOALS		
	P	W	D	L	F	A	PTS
England	3	2	1	0	4	0	5
Uruguay	3	1	2	0	2	1	4
Mexico	3	0	2	1	1	3	2
France	3	0	1	2	2	5	1

Group II

West Germany 5, Switzerland 0 (HT 3–0)
Argentina 2, Spain 1 (HT 0–0)
Spain 2, Switzerland 1 (HT 0–1)
Argentina 0, West Germany 0 (HT 0–0)
Argentina 2, Switzerland 0 (HT 0–0)
West Germany 2, Spain 1 (HT 1–1)

					GOALS		
	P	W	D	L	F	A	PTS
West Germany	3	2	1	0	7	1	5
Argentina	3	2	1	0	4	1	5
Spain	3	1	0	2	4	5	2
Switzerland	3	0	0	3	1	9	0

Group III

Brazil 2, Bulgaria 0 (HT 1–0)
Portugal 3, Hungary 1 (HT 1–0)
Hungary 3, Brazil 1 (HT 1–1)
Portugal 3, Bulgaria 0 (HT 2–0)
Portugal 3, Brazil 1 (HT 2–0)
Hungary 3, Bulgaria 1 (HT 2–1)

					GOALS		
	P	W	D	L	F	A	PTS
Portugal	3	3	0	0	9	2	6
Hungary	3	2	0	1	7	5	4
Brazil	3	1	0	2	4	6	2
Bulgaria	3	0	0	3	1	8	0

Group IV

Russia 3, North Korea 0 (HT 2–0)
Italy 2, Chile 0 (HT 1–0)
Chile 1, North Korea 1 (HT 1–0)
Russia 1, Italy 0 (HT 0–0)
North Korea 1, Italy 0 (HT 1–0)
Russia 2, Chile 1 (HT 1–1)

					GOALS		
	P	W	D	L	F	A	PTS
Russia	3	3	0	0	6	1	6
North Korea	3	1	1	1	2	4	3
Italy	3	1	0	2	2	2	2
Chile	3	0	1	2	2	5	1

Quarter-finals

Wembley

England 1
Banks; Cohen, Wilson; Stiles, Charlton, J., Moore; Ball, Hurst, Charlton, R., Hunt, Peters.

Argentina 0
Roma; Ferreiro, Perfumo, Albrecht, Marzolini; Gonzalez, Rattin, Onega; Solari, Artime, Mas.

SCORER
Hurst for England
(HT 0–0)

Hillsborough

West Germany 4 Tilkowski; Hottges, Weber, Schulz, Schnellinger; Beckenbauer, Haller, Overath; Seeler, Held, Emmerich.	Uruguay 0 Mazurkiewicz; Troche, Ubinas, Gonçalves, Manicera, Caetano; Salva, Rocha; Silva, Cortes, Perez.
SCORERS Held, Beckenbauer, Seeler, Haller for West Germany (HT 1–0)	

Everton

Portugal 5 José Pereira; Morais, Baptista, Vicente, Hilario; Graça, Coluna; José Augusto, Eusebio, Torres, Simoes.	North Korea 3 Li Chan Myung; Rim Yung Sum, Shin Yung Kyoo, Ha Jung Won, O Yoon Kyung; Pak Seung Jin, Jon Seung Hwi; Han Bong Zin, Pak Doo Ik, Li Dong Woon, Yang Sung Kook.
SCORERS Eusebio (4) (2 penalties), José Augusto for Portugal (HT 2–3)	Pak Seung Jin, Yang Sung Kook, Li Dong Woon for North Korea

Sunderland

Russia 2 Yachine; Ponomarev, Chesternijev, Voronin, Danilov; Sabo, Khusainov; Chislenko, Banichevski, Malafeev Porkujan.	Hungary 1 Gelei; Matrai, Kaposzta, Meszoly, Sipos, Szepesi; Nagy, Albert, Rakosi; Bene, Farkas.
SCORERS Chislenko, Porkujan for Russia (HT 1–0)	Bene for Hungary

Semi-finals

Everton

West Germany 2 Tilkowski; Hottges, Weber, Schulz, Schnellinger; Beckenbauer, Haller, Overath; Seeler, Held, Emmerich.	Russia 1 Yachine; Ponomarev, Chesternijev, Voronin, Danilov; Sabo, Khusainov; Chislenko, Banichevski, Malafeev, Porkujan.
SCORERS Haller, Beckenbauer for West Germany (HT 1–0)	Porkujan for Russia

Wembley

England 2 Banks; Cohen, Wilson; Stiles, Charlton, J., Moore; Ball, Hurst, Charlton, R., Hunt, Peters.	Portugal 1 José Pereira; Festa, Baptista, José Carlos, Hilario; Graça, Coluna, José Augusto; Eusebio, Torres, Simoes.
SCORERS Charlton, R (2) for England (HT 1–0)	Eusebio (penalty) for Portugal

Third place match

Wembley

Portugal 2 José Pereira; Festa, Baptista, José Carlos, Hilario; Graça, Coluna, José Augusto; Eusebio, Torres, Simoes	Russia 1 Yachine; Ponomarev, Khurtsilava, Korneev, Danilov; Voronin, Sichinava; Metreveli, Malafeev, Banichevski, Serebrianikov.
SCORERS Eusebio (penalty), Torres for Portugal (HT 1–1)	Malafeev for Russia

Final

Wembley

England 4 (after extra time)	West Germany 2
Banks; Cohen, Wilson; Stiles, Charlton, J., Moore; Ball, Hurst, Hunt, Charlton, R., Peters.	Tilkowski; Hottges, Schulz, Weber, Schnellinger; Haller, Beckenbauer, Overath; Seeler, Held, Emmerich.

SCORERS

Hurst (3), Peters for England (HT 1–1)	Haller, Weber for West Germany

Mexico 1970

Group I

Mexico 0, Russia 0 (HT 0–0)
Belgium 3, El Salvador 0 (HT 1–0)
Russia 4, Belgium 1 (HT 1–0)
Mexico 4, El Salvador 0 (HT 1–0)
Russia 2, El Salvador 0 (HT 0–0)
Mexico 1, Belgium 0 (HT 1–0)

					GOALS		
	P	W	D	L	F	A	PTS
Russia	3	2	1	0	6	1	5
Mexico	3	2	1	0	5	0	5
Belgium	3	1	0	2	4	5	2
El Salvador	3	0	0	3	0	9	0

Group II

Uruguay 2, Israel 0 (HT 1–0)
Italy 1, Sweden 0 (HT 1–0)
Uruguay 0, Italy 0 (HT 0–0)
Sweden 1, Israel 1 (HT 0–0)
Sweden 1, Uruguay 0 (HT 0–0)
Italy 0, Israel 0 (HT 0–0)

					GOALS		
	P	W	D	L	F	A	PTS
Italy	3	1	2	0	1	0	4
Uruguay	3	1	1	1	2	1	3
Sweden	3	1	1	1	2	2	3
Israel	3	0	2	1	1	3	2

Group III

England 1, Romania 0 (HT 0–0)
Brazil 4, Czechoslovakia 1 (HT 1–1)
Romania 2, Czechoslovakia 1 (HT 0–1)
Brazil 1, England 0 (HT 0–0)
Brazil 3, Romania 2 (HT 2–1)
England 1, Czechoslovakia 0 (HT 0–0)

					GOALS		
	P	W	D	L	F	A	PTS
Brazil	3	3	0	0	8	3	6
England	3	2	0	1	2	1	4
Romania	3	1	0	2	4	5	2
Czechoslovakia	3	0	0	3	2	7	0

Group IV

Peru 3, Bulgaria 2 (HT 0–1)
West Germany 2, Morocco 1 (HT 0–1)
Peru 3, Morocco 0 (HT 0–0)
West Germany 5, Bulgaria 2 (HT 2–1)
West Germany 3, Peru 1 (HT 3–1)
Morocco 1, Bulgaria 1 (HT 1–0)

					GOALS		
	P	W	D	L	F	A	PTS
West Germany	3	3	0	0	10	4	6
Peru	3	2	0	1	7	5	4
Bulgaria	3	0	1	2	5	9	1
Morocco	3	0	1	2	2	6	1

Quarter-finals

León

West Germany 3
(after extra time)
Maier; Schnellinger, Vogts, Hottges (Schulz); Beckenbauer, Overath, Seeler; Libuda (Grabowski), Muller, Loehr.

England 2

Bonetti; Newton; Cooper; Mullery, Labone, Moore; Lee, Ball, Hurst, Charlton (Bell), Peters (Hunter).

SCORERS
Beckenbauer, Seeler, Muller for West Germany

Mullery, Peters for England

(HT 0–1)

Guadalajara

Brazil 4
Felix; Carlos Alberto, Brito, Piazza, Marco Antonio; Clodoaldo, Gerson (Paulo Cesar); Jairzinho (Roberto), Tostão, Pelé, Rivelino.

Peru 2
Rubiños; Campos, Fernandez, Chumpitaz, Fuentes; Mifflin, Challe; Baylon (Sotil), Perico Leon (Eladio Reyes), Cubillas, Gallardo.

SCORERS
Rivelino, Tostão (2), Jairzinho for Brazil

Gallardo, Cubillas for Peru

(HT 2–1)

Toluca

Italy 4
Albertosi; Burgnich, Cera, Rosato, Facchetti; Bertini, Mazzola (Rivera), De Sisti; Domenghini (Gori), Boninsegna, Riva.

Mexico 1
Calderon; Vantolra, Pena, Guzman, Perez; Gonzalez (Borja), Pulido, Munguia (Diaz); Valdivia, Fragoso, Padilla.

SCORERS
Domenghini, Riva (2), Rivera for Italy

Gonzalez for Mexico

(HT 1–1)

Mexico City

Uruguay 1
(after extra time)
Mazurkiewicz; Ubinas, Ancheta, Matosas, Mujica; Maneiro, Cortes, Montero Castillo; Cubilla, Fontes (Gomez), Morales (Esparrago).

Russia 0

Kavazashvili; Dzodzuashvili, Afonin, Khurtsilava (Logofet), Chesternijev; Muntijan, Asatiani (Kiselev), Kaplichni; Evriuzhkinzin, Bychevetz, Khmelnitzki.

SCORER
Esparrago for Uruguay
(HT 0–0)

Semi-finals

Mexico City

Italy 4
(after extra time)
Albertosi; Cera, Burgnich, Bertini, Rosato (Poletti), Facchetti; Domenghini, Mazzola (Rivera), De Sisti; Boninsegna, Riva.

West Germany 3

Maier; Schnellinger; Vogts, Schulz, Beckenbauer, Patzke (Held); Seeler, Overath; Grabowski, Muller, Loehr (Libuda).

SCORERS
Boninsegna, Burgnich, Riva, Rivera for Italy
(HT 1–0)

Schnellinger, Muller (2) for West Germany

Guadalajara

Brazil 3
Felix; Carlos Alberto, Brito, Piazza, Everaldo; Clodoaldo, Gerson; Jairzinho, Tostão, Pelé, Rivelino.

Uruguay 1
Mazurkiewicz; Ubinas, Ancheta, Matosas, Mujica; Montero Castillo, Cortes, Fontes; Cubilla, Maneiro (Esparrago), Morales.

SCORERS
Clodoaldo, Jairzinho, Rivelino for Brazil
(HT 1–1)

Cubilla for Uruguay

Third place match

Mexico City

West Germany 1
Wolter; Schnellinger (Lorenz); Patzke, Fichtel, Weber, Vogts; Seeler, Overath; Libuda (Loehr), Muller, Held.

Uruguay 0
Mazurkiewicz; Ubinas, Ancheta, Matosas, Mujica; Montero Castillo, Cortes, Fontes (Sandoval); Cubilla, Maneiro (Esparrago), Morales.

SCORER
Overath for West Germany
(HT 1–0)

Final

Mexico City

Brazil 4
Felix; Carlos Alberto, Brito, Piazza, Everaldo; Clodoaldo, Gerson; Jairzinho, Tostão, Pelé, Rivelino.

Italy 1
Albertosi; Cera; Burgnich, Bertini (Juliano), Rosato, Facchetti; Domenghini, Mazzola, De Sisti; Boninsegna (Rivera), Riva.

SCORERS
Pelé, Gerson, Jairzinho, Carlos Alberto for Brazil
(HT 1–1)

Boninsegna for Italy

West Germany 1974

Group I

West Germany 1, Chile 0 (HT 0–0)
East Germany 2, Australia 0 (HT 0–0)
West Germany 3, Australia 0 (HT 2–0)
East Germany 1, Chile 1 (HT 0–0)
East Germany 1, West Germany 0 (HT 1–0)
Chile 0, Australia 0 (HT 0–0)

					GOALS		
	P	W	D	L	F	A	PTS
East Germany	3	2	1	0	4	1	5
West Germany	3	2	0	1	4	1	4
Chile	3	0	2	1	1	2	1
Australia	3	0	1	2	0	5	1

Group II

Brazil 0, Yugoslavia 0 (HT 0–0)
Scotland 2, Zaire 0 (HT 2–0)
Brazil 0, Scotland 0 (HT 0–0)
Yugoslavia 9, Zaire 0 (HT 6–0)
Scotland 1, Yugoslavia 1 (HT 0–0)
Brazil 3, Zaire 0 (HT 1–0)

					GOALS		
	P	W	D	L	F	A	PTS
Yugoslavia	3	1	2	0	10	1	4
Brazil	3	1	2	0	3	0	4
Scotland	3	1	2	0	3	1	4
Zaire	3	0	0	3	0	14	0

Group III

Holland 2, Uruguay 0 (HT 1–0)
Sweden 0, Bulgaria 0 (HT 0–0)
Holland 0, Sweden 0 (HT 0–0)
Bulgaria 1, Uruguay 1 (HT 0–0)
Holland 4, Bulgaria 1 (HT 2–0)
Sweden 3, Uruguay 0 (HT 0–0)

					GOALS		
	P	W	D	L	F	A	PTS
Holland	3	2	1	0	6	1	5
Sweden	3	1	2	0	3	0	4
Bulgaria	3	0	2	1	2	5	2
Uruguay	3	0	1	2	1	6	1

Group IV

Italy 3, Haiti 1 (HT 0–0)
Poland 3, Argentina 2 (HT 2–0)
Italy 1, Argentina 1 (HT 1–1)
Poland 7, Haiti 0 (HT 5–0)
Argentina 4, Haiti 1 (HT 2–0)
Poland 2, Italy 1 (HT 2–0)

					GOALS		
	P	W	D	L	F	A	PTS
Poland	3	3	0	0	12	3	6
Argentina	3	1	1	1	7	5	3
Italy	3	1	1	1	5	4	3
Haiti	3	0	0	3	2	14	0

Group A

Brazil 1, East Germany 0 (HT 0–0)
Holland 4, Argentina 0 (HT 2–0)
Holland 2, East Germany 0 (HT 1–0)
Brazil 2, Argentina 1 (HT 1–1)
Holland 2, Brazil 0 (HT 0–0)
Argentina 1, East Germany 1 (HT 1–1)

					GOALS		
	P	W	D	L	F	A	PTS
Holland	3	3	0	0	8	0	6
Brazil	3	2	0	1	3	3	4
East Germany	3	0	1	2	1	4	1
Argentina	3	0	1	2	2	7	1

Group B

Poland 1, Sweden 0 (HT 1–0)
West Germany 2, Yugoslavia 0 (HT 1–0)
Poland 2, Yugoslavia 1 (HT 1–1)
West Germany 4, Sweden 2 (HT 0–1)
Sweden 2, Yugoslavia 1 (HT 0–0)
West Germany 1, Poland 0 (HT 0–0)

					GOALS		
	P	W	D	L	F	A	PTS
West Germany	3	3	0	0	7	2	6
Poland	3	2	0	1	3	2	4
Sweden	3	1	0	2	4	6	2
Yugoslavia	3	0	0	3	2	6	0

Third place match

Munich

Poland 1
Tomaszewski; Szymanowski, Gorgon, Zmuda, Musial; Kasperczak (Cmikiewicz), Deyna, Masczyk; Lato, Szarmach (Kapka), Gadocha.

Brazil 0
Leao; Ze Maria, Alfredo, Marinho, M., Marinho, F.; Paulo Cesar Carpeggiani, Rivelino, Ademir da Guia (Mirandinha); Valdomiro, Jairzinho, Dirceu.

SCORER
Lato for Poland
(HT 0–0)

Final

Munich

West Germany 2
Maier; Beckenbauer; Vogts, Schwarzenbeck, Breitner; Bonhof, Hoeness, Overath; Grabowski, Muller, Holzenbein.

Holland 1
Jongbloed; Suurbier, Rijsbergen, (De Jong), Haan, Krol; Jansen, Neeskens, Van Hanegem; Rep, Cruyff, Rensenbrink (Van de Kerkhof, R.).

SCORERS
Breitner (penalty), Muller for West Germany

Neeskens (penalty) for Holland

(HT 2–1)

Argentina 1978

Group I

Argentina 2, Hungary 1 (HT 1–1)
Italy 2, France 1 (HT 1–1)
Argentina 2, France 1 (HT 1–0)
Italy 3, Hungary 1 (HT 2–0)
Italy 1, Argentina 0 (HT 2–0)
France 3, Hungary 1 (HT 3–1)

					GOALS		
	P	W	D	L	F	A	PTS
Italy	3	3	0	0	6	2	6
Argentina	3	2	0	1	4	3	4
France	3	1	0	2	5	5	2
Hungary	3	0	0	3	3	8	0

Group II

West Germany 0, Poland 0 (HT 0–0)
Tunisia 3, Mexico 1 (HT 0–1)
Poland 1, Tunisia 0 (HT 1–0)
West Germany 6, Mexico 0 (HT 4–0)
Poland 3, Mexico 1 (HT 1–0)
West Germany 0, Tunisia 0 (HT 0–0)

					GOALS		
	P	W	D	L	F	A	PTS
Poland	3	2	1	0	4	1	5
West Germany	3	1	2	0	6	0	4
Tunisia	3	1	1	1	3	2	3
Mexico	3	0	0	3	2	12	0

Group III

Austria 2, Spain 1 (HT 1–1)
Sweden 1, Brazil 1 (HT 1–1)
Austria 1, Sweden 0 (HT 1–0)
Brazil 0, Spain 0 (HT 0–0)
Spain 1, Sweden 0 (HT 0–0)
Brazil 1, Austria 0 (HT 1–0)

					GOALS		
	P	W	D	L	F	A	PTS
Austria	3	2	0	1	3	2	4
Brazil	3	1	2	0	2	1	4
Spain	3	1	1	1	2	2	3
Sweden	3	0	1	2	1	3	1

Group IV

Peru 3, Scotland 1 (HT 1–1)
Holland 3, Iran 0 (HT 1–0)
Scotland 1, Iran 1 (HT 1–0)
Holland 0, Peru 0 (HT 0–0)
Peru 4, Iran 1 (HT 3–1)
Scotland 3, Holland 2 (HT 1–1)

					GOALS		
	P	W	D	L	F	A	PTS
Peru	3	2	1	0	7	2	5
Holland	3	1	1	1	5	3	3
Scotland	3	1	1	1	5	6	3
Iran	3	0	1	2	2	8	1

Group A

Italy 0, West Germany 0 (HT 0–0)
Holland 5, Austria 1 (HT 3–0)
Italy 1, Austria 0 (HT 1–0)
Austria 3, West Germany 2 (HT 0–1)
Holland 2, Italy 1 (HT 0–1)
Holland 2, West Germany 2 (HT 1–1)

					GOALS		
	P	W	D	L	F	A	PTS
Holland	3	2	1	0	9	4	5
Italy	3	1	1	1	2	2	3
West Germany	3	0	2	1	4	5	2
Austria	3	1	0	2	4	8	2

Group B

Argentina 2, Poland 0 (HT 1–0)
Brazil 3, Peru 0 (HT 2–0)
Argentina 0, Brazil 0 (HT 0–0)
Poland 1, Peru 0 (HT 0–0)
Brazil 3, Poland 1 (HT 1–1)
Argentina 6, Peru 0 (HT 2–0)

					GOALS		
	P	W	D	L	F	A	PTS
Argentina	3	2	1	0	8	0	5
Brazil	3	2	1	0	6	1	5
Poland	3	1	0	2	2	5	2
Peru	3	0	0	3	0	10	0

Third place match

Buenos Aires

Brazil 2
Leao; Nelinho, Oscar, Amaral, Neto; Cerezo (Rivelino), Batista, Dirceu; Gil (Reinaldo), Mendonça, Roberto.

Italy 1
Zoff; Scirea, Gentile, Cuccureddu, Cabrini; Maldera, Antognoni (Sala, C.), Sala, P.; Causio; Rossi, Bettega.

SCORERS
Nelinho, Dirceu for Brazil
Causio for Italy
(HT 0–1)

Final

Buenos Aires

Argentina 3
(after extra time)
Fillol; Olguin, Galvan, Passarella, Tarantini; Ardiles (Larrosa), Gallego, Kempes; Bertoni, Luque, Ortiz (Houseman).

Holland 1
Jongbloed; Krol, Poortvliet, Brandts, Jansen (Suurbier); Van de Kerkhof, W., Neeskens, Haan; Rep (Nanninga), Rensenbrink, Van de Kerkhof, R.

SCORERS
Kempes (2), Bertoni for Argentina
Nanninga for Holland
(HT 1–0 FT 1–1)

Spain 1982

Group I

Italy 0, Poland 0
Cameroons 0, Peru 0
Italy 1, Peru 1
Cameroons 0, Poland 0
Poland 5, Peru 1
Cameroons 1, Italy 1

	P	W	D	L	GOALS F	GOALS A	PTS
Poland	3	1	2	0	5	1	4
Italy	3	0	3	0	2	2	3
Cameroons	3	0	3	0	1	1	3
Peru	3	0	2	1	2	6	2

Group II

Algeria 2, West Germany 1
Austria 1, Chile 0
West Germany 4, Chile 1
Austria 2, Algeria 0
Algeria 3, Chile 2
West Germany 1, Austria 0

	P	W	D	L	GOALS F	GOALS A	PTS
West Germany	3	2	0	1	6	3	4
Austria	3	2	0	1	3	1	4
Algeria	3	2	0	1	5	5	4
Chile	3	0	0	3	3	8	0

Group III

Belgium 1, Argentina 0
Hungary 10, El Salvador 1
Argentina 4, Hungary 1
Belgium 1, El Salvador 0
Belgium 1, Hungary 1
Argentina 2, El Salvador 0

					GOALS		
	P	W	D	L	F	A	PTS
Belgium	3	2	1	0	3	1	5
Argentina	3	2	0	1	6	2	4
Hungary	3	1	1	1	12	6	3
El Salvador	3	0	0	3	1	13	0

Group IV

England 3, France 1
Czechoslovakia 1, Kuwait 1
England 2, Czechoslovakia 0
France 4, Kuwait 1
France 1, Czechoslovakia 1
England 1, Kuwait 0

					GOALS		
	P	W	D	L	F	A	PTS
England	3	3	0	0	6	1	6
France	3	1	1	1	6	5	3
Czechoslovakia	3	0	2	1	2	4	2
Kuwait	3	0	1	2	2	6	1

Group V

Spain 1, Honduras 1
Yugoslavia 0, Northern Ireland 0
Spain 2, Yugoslavia 1
Honduras 1, Northern Ireland 1
Yugoslavia 1, Honduras 0
Northern Ireland 1, Spain 0

					GOALS		
	P	W	D	L	F	A	PTS
Northern Ireland	3	1	2	0	2	1	4
Spain	3	1	1	1	3	3	3
Yugoslavia	3	1	1	1	2	2	3
Honduras	3	0	2	1	2	3	2

Group VI

Brazil 2, Russia 1
Scotland 5, New Zealand 2
Brazil 4, Scotland 1
Russia 3, New Zealand 0
Scotland 2, Russia 2
Brazil 4, New Zealand 0

					GOALS		
	P	W	D	L	F	A	PTS
Brazil	3	3	0	0	10	2	6
Russia	3	1	1	1	6	4	3
Scotland	3	1	1	1	8	8	3
New Zealand	3	0	0	3	2	12	0

Group A

Barcelona

Poland 3, Belgium 0
Russia 1, Belgium 0
Russia 0, Poland 0

					GOALS		
	P	W	D	L	F	A	PTS
Poland	2	1	1	0	3	0	3
Russia	2	1	1	0	1	0	3
Belgium	2	0	0	2	0	4	0

Group B

Madrid

England 0, West Germany 0
Spain 1, West Germany 2
Spain 0, England 0

					GOALS		
	P	W	D	L	F	A	PTS
West Germany	2	1	1	0	2	1	3
England	2	0	2	0	0	0	2
Spain	2	0	1	1	1	2	1

Group C

Barcelona

Italy 2, Argentina 1
Brazil 3, Argentina 1
Italy 3, Brazil 2

					GOALS		
	P	W	D	L	F	A	PTS
Italy	2	2	0	0	5	3	4
Brazil	2	1	0	1	5	4	2
Argentina	2	0	0	2	2	5	0

Group D

Madrid

France 1, Austria 0
Austria 2, Northern Ireland 2
France 4, Northern Ireland 1

					GOALS		
	P	W	D	L	F	A	PTS
France	2	2	0	0	5	1	4
Austria	2	0	1	1	2	3	1
Northern Ireland	2	0	1	1	3	6	1

Semi-finals

Barcelona

Italy 2
Zoff; Scirea; Bergomi, Collovati, Cabrini; Tardelli, Oriali, Antognoni (Marini), Conti; Graziani (Altobelli), Rossi.

Poland 0
Mlynarczyk; Dziuba, Zmuda, Janes, Majewski; Matysik, Buncol, Ciolek (Palasz), Kupcewicz; Lato, Smolarek (Kusto).

SCORERS
Rossi (2)
(HT 0–0)

Seville

West Germany 3
Schumacher; Stielike; K. Foerster, B. Foerster, Briegel (Rummenigge); Breitner, Magath (Hrubesch), Dremmler; Littbarski, Fischer.

France 3
Ettori; Amoros, Trésor, Janvion, Bossis; Tigana, Genghini (Battiston (Lopez)), Platini, Giresse; Rocheteau, Six.

SCORERS
Littbarski, Rummenigge, Fischer for West Germany

Platini (penalty), Trésor, Giresse for France

(HT 1–1, FT 1–1)
West Germany won by five penalties to four.

Third place match

Alicante

Poland 3
Mlynarczyk; Dziuba, Janes, Zmuda, Majewski; Lato, Buncol, Kupcewicz, Matysik, (Wojicki); Boniek, Szarmach.

France 2
Castaneda; Amoros, Trésor, Mahut, Janvion (Lopez); Tigana (Six), Girard, Larios; Couriol, Soler, Bellone.

SCORERS
Szarmach, Majewski, Kupcewicz for Poland
(HT 2–1)

Girard, Couriol for France

Final

Madrid

Italy 3
Zoff; Scirea; Bergomi, Collovati, Gentile, Cabrini; Conti, Tardelli, Oriali; Rossi, Graziani (Altobelli (Causio)).

West Germany 1
Schumacher; Stielike; Kaltz, K. Foerster, B. Foerster, Briegel; Dremmler (Hrubesch), Breitner; Littbarski, Fischer, Rummenigge (Muller).

SCORERS
Rossi, Tardelli, Altobelli for Italy
(HT 0–0)

Breitner for West Germany

Index of Players

Major references are indicated by **Bold Type**. Page numbers in *italics* refer to the team lists in the World Cup Results section.

Abbreviations used in the index:

Arg.	Argentina	It.	Italy
Aus.	Austria	Mex.	Mexico
Belg.	Belgium	Pol.	Poland
Br.	Brazil	Scot.	Scotland
Cz.	Czechoslovakia	Sp.	Spain
Eng.	England	Urug.	Uruguay
Fr.	France	U.S.	United States
Germ.	Germany	W. Germ.	West Germany
Hung.	Hungary		

Also by Brian Glanville

THE PUFFIN BOOK OF FOOTBALL

In 1872, two thousand people turned up to watch the first ever English Cup Final. In 1982 a thousand million people around the world watched the World Cup in Spain on television. What started as a gentleman's hobby has become a spectacle that unites people of all nations. This is a splendidly readable account of the history of soccer, of how it has developed, what it has become and what may or may not happen to it in the future.

A BOOK OF FOOTBALLERS

Using his incomparable worldwide knowledge of the game, Brian Glanville has compiled an alphabetical guide to great footballers, past and present, European and South American. An invaluable book for football lovers.

THE PUFFIN BMX HANDBOOK

Written by the editorial team of Britain's leading magazine, *BMX Action Bike*, this handbook is essential reading for both beginners and experts. Apart from tips about choosing the right machine, accessories and clothes for safety, there are also training files and detailed instructions on the pleasures and pitfalls of all the techniques, tricks, stunts and racing thrills that add up to make the total picture of a true BMX rider.

CHIPS, COMPUTERS AND ROBOTS

Judy Allen

At the heart of the modern electronic revolution – which has made possible the computer and the calculator, robots and video games – lies the chip. But what is the chip exactly? How does it work – and what can it do? The answers are here, in this straightforward, fascinating explanation of microtechnology from the chip to robots and beyond.

MICRO GAMES

Patrick Bossert and Philippa Dickinson

In 1981 Patrick Bossert showed the world how to crack the cube in his bestselling book, *You Can do the Cube*. Now he turns his attention to the micro-computer and has devised a great collection of games listings. There is a death-defying bomb run, a hair-raising car race, a bat-and-ball game, fiendish puzzles to work out and many more. All the games need lightning reactions, quick thinking or good powers of observation – and all will help you understand your computer that little bit better.

AND IN PUFFIN PLUS (*for older readers*)

FROM SCHOOLBOY TO SUPERSTAR

Patrick Barclay

What does it take to become a professional footballer? And just how do you set about joining a club? Through a series of interviews with stars like Steve Coppell, Dennis Tueart and Sammy Lee, Patrick Barclay shows what you need to make the grade . . . and, just as important, how to ensure that your life doesn't fall apart if you don't quite make it as a footballer.

Heard about the Puffin Club?

. . . it's a way of finding out more about Puffin books and authors, of winning prizes (in competitions), sharing jokes, a secret code, and perhaps seeing your name in print! When you join you get a copy of our magazine, *Puffin Post*, sent to you four times a year, a badge and a membership book.
For details of subscription and an application form, send a stamped addressed envelope to:

The Puffin Club Dept A
Penguin Books Limited
Bath Road
Harmondsworth
Middlesex UB7 ODA

and if you live in Australia, please write to;

The Australian Puffin Club
Penguin Books Australia Limited
P.O. Box 257
Ringwood
Victoria 3134